WALKING THE LINE

ENJOYING DISUSED RAILWAYS AND TRAMWAYS IN BRITAIN

ANTHONY BURTON

WALKING THE LINE

ENJOYING DISUSED RAILWAYS AND TRAMWAYS IN BRITAIN

Blandford Press

Poole

First published in the U.K. by Blandford Press
Link House, West Street, Poole, Dorset, BH15 1LL

ISBN 0 7137 1554 5

British Library Cataloguing in Publication Data

Burton, Anthony
    Walking the line : enjoying disused railway
    & tramways in Britain.
    1. Railroads – Great Britain – Abandonment
    I. Title
    385'.0941   HE3014

Front jacket The Glen Ogle
Trail

Back jacket Highgate houses
beside the Parkland Walk;
pub sign at Blackmoor Gate
on the former Lynton and
Barnstaple Light Railway;
The railway track on the
cliffs of Portland.

Title spread Not just a track
through the fields, but the
last remains of a once-busy
railway. This is part of the
Pencaitland Walk in
Scotland.

Conceived, edited, and designed by Curtis Garratt Limited
The Old Vicarage, Horton cum Studley, Oxford, OX9 1BT

Typeset in 10/11pt Times Roman
by Oxford Print Associates

Printed in Spain by Grijelmo S.A., Bilbao

CONTENTS

FIRST STEPS

The British have various views about their railways. Some take extreme positions: the commuter who catches the 08.15 into Waterloo every morning and the 17.40 out again every evening will often be heard cursing the train; while, at the other end of the scale, the small and even large boys (never it seems small or large girls) who congregate at the ends of draughty platforms scrupulously recording numbers in notebooks can become besotted with all aspects of railway life. Most of us come somewhere between, being on the whole in favour of railways, but reserving a special affection for those of the Golden Age. For it has to be admitted that railways are not what they were. Romantic steam has given way to prosaic diesel and electric, and the great rail network built up by the Victorians has shrivelled and shrunk. In 1952 there were over 19 000 miles of track in use, 8212 stations, and 956 marshalling yards: twenty years later the track length was down to just over 11 000 miles, there were only 2735 stations and a paltry fifty-three marshalling yards. What had happened between can be summed up in one name – Beeching. Whether you describe him as one eminent railway writer did recently as '. . . the greatest railwayman since Brunel . . .', the man who had the courage to prune away the dead branches and thus saved the railway tree, or whether you think of him as the mad axeman lopping away viciously at the living plant, it cannot be denied that he left his mark on the railways. He also, of course, left 8000 miles of railway to decay – tracks pulled up, sleepers dragged out, equipment removed. It is with those 'lost miles' that this book will be chiefly – but not entirely – concerned.

A tiny proportion of those abandoned lines has been brought back to life by enthusiasts. There are now more than sixty preserved lines where the steam locomotive reigns supreme in all its manifestations from the famous narrow gauges of Wales to the great main line engines. The lines themselves show equal diversity, from small industrial routes to recreations of branch line and even main line life. But these are not our concern here, for these represent only around 2 per cent of the lines abandoned under the Beeching Plan. It is at the rest, abandoned but not forgotten, that we shall be looking.

Take out any of the 1:50 000 Ordnance Survey maps and you will probably find sketched across it something that resembles a series of hairy caterpillars joined by dotted lines, with somewhere the faint legend 'disused railway'. The caterpillars represent embankments and cuttings, the dotted lines the level track. Trains may no longer run over the metals, but the old routes have not yet faded into oblivion. In straight lines or long, sweeping curves they still form a recognizable pattern in the British landscape. Looking at the OS sheet 174, covering the area to the south of my own home, just such a line appears as a continuous route stretching

Opposite The building of a railway could involve civil engineering work on a massive scale, which dramatically altered the appearance of the country-side. Certainly no-one could mistake this deep cutting through a hill on the Tissington Trail for a natural feature.

Upton Station still retains much of its original character, even though the track has long gone and the buildings have been converted into a private house.

from Didcot to Newbury and even a quick glance over the route on the map gives an immediate indication of why old railways hold out promises of, at the very least, a different way of seeing the countryside. The line is shown as leaving Didcot on an embankment which is followed by a cutting and then by a long, continuous bank that runs all the way to Upton, where it disappears into a cutting in which it remains for several miles before emerging on the flat to swing down towards Compton. The line of the railway is, then, in a sense a very unnatural line, compared with the myriad footpaths that cross the same area, running along ridges or dipping into hollows. The older paths simply sit on the landscape, adapting to the existing structure of the country: the railway builders rearranged the landscape to suit their own designs. This is true of virtually all railways, and forms a part of their special appeal. To understand it more completely, we have to take the map out of the study and set off to look at the track on the ground.

Many people probably see this track for the first time, even if they are not especially aware of its significance, when they take the train from Didcot to Paddington. As they pull out of the station on their way east, they will see the embankment diverging away to the south in a sharp curve – after that the London train goes on its way, leaving the old line to its own devices. Lines such as this can easily get lost in their passage through towns – the track built over, crossings and bridges removed, cuttings filled in. Our line has not altogether avoided that fate but, at Northbourne on the edge of

Didcot, the local authority has taken it into its care. A cutting has been turned into a short, linear park in which a footpath meanders in a manner that the old rails never did. There is still a remembrance of the past, however, in the path itself which is probably described officially as gravel but which consists not just of stones but of veritable rocks, as substantial as any ballast could ever have been. The line passes under a red brick bridge, its arch blackened by the smoke of thousands of locomotives and it is a poor, unromantic sort of soul that does not feel a touch of nostalgia nor hear the whisper of a distant steam whistle hanging on the breeze.

Beyond the cutting, the line does one of its temporary disappearing acts beneath a new housing estate, to re-emerge on that long, straight bank that bisects the villages of East and West Hagbourne. At once, the special nature of the railway asserts itself. To those travelling at the 'natural' ground level, the bank forms an obstruction, blocking the view; while the top of the bank itself provides just the opposite, a splendid vantage point from which to see the surrounding country. Both villages are in sight, as is the path which pierces the bank and along which the late lamented of churchless West Hagbourne have for centuries been carried for internment in the neighbouring village to the east. The view on offer is a panorama from above rooftop level and, indeed, roofs now take on a new significance. To the east, a fine range of barns has been converted to 'executive housing' and, however well they might look from ground level, from up on the bank they appear anachronistic. Glass lights let into the roofs quite destroy the character of the old farm buildings, in contrast to another range of barns to the west. Ramshackle these latter may be, but they are still in use and their essential characteristics of structure and material remain unchanged. And it is not just the buildings close at hand that are revealed from up here on the bank. Distant prospects are opened, wider views obtained than are possible from more conventional footpaths. The structure of the land itself becomes clearer, patterns that were just coloured lines on a map take on a physical reality.

Ahead the line rises towards Blewbury Down, through which the railway must make a passage. But first there is a pause – or rather there was a pause – in the form of Upton Station, now a private house. It was never a major feature on the line, more a halt than a station but, however humble, it still earned a place in that great compendium of railway facts – *The Railway Clearing House Handbook of Railway Stations*. The volume for 1904 informs you that Upton Station was then the property of the Great Western Railway, that it was equipped to handle both goods and passengers; that it would take livestock, horse boxes and prize cattle vans, but would be forced to turn away furniture vans, portable engines, and machines on wheels. The goods traffic must also have been somewhat limited as the total crane lifting power was merely one ton. The Handbook notes that most companies had more powerful travelling cranes '. . . which can be removed from one Station to another as circumstances require. . . '. It was not, however, very wise to rely on *that*. Today, looking at the trim little house, it is still possible to people it in imagination with a few waiting farmers and a clutter of milk churns. On market days, the station would have been enlivened by the noise of cattle and sheep. But, if traffic was light, you may be quite sure the station was immaculate, preserving the high standards of 'God's Wonderful Railway'.

Beyond the station, the line begins to drive through the hills in a deep cutting. You can look down on the cutting from an adjoining footpath but, scramble down into it, and you find the world of the embankment has been reversed. Where the latter offered a bird's-eye view of the surrounding countryside, the cutting all but obliterates it. The steep sides close in on the walker, creating a narrow corridor with little to hint at what is going on in the world outside the cutting. There are compensations though, for the cutting has created its own world. Since the last train ran through in 1964, vegetation has begun to grow thick and lush, protected from the harsher downland winds. Then, where the sides are too steep to support vegetation, the structure of the land is revealed: bands of crumbling chalk poke through the cutting side, like a geological layer cake. Man has also found a new use for the old cutting. The local gun club meets here and the whole area is littered with bright red and orange cartridge cases and the shattered discs of clay pigeon shoots. This has not deterred the local rabbit population from making their own homes in the banks.

The cutting is also a good place to view the world of the railway builder. Deep cuttings demand tall bridges and there are a number of handsome examples along the way, including a fine skew bridge. Where railway and established road met at an angle, the engineers were faced with two alternatives: they could put a couple of sharp bends in the road so that the bridge could cross at right angles – easy for the engineer, but a confounded nuisance to road users, or they could build the bridge on the skew. This involved laying the bricks on a pattern formed of horizontals and diagonals rather than the conventional horizontals and verticals. The result is a truly elegant piece of bridge building and it can be seen at Tile Barn bridge – where the nearest barn has, intriguingly, no sign of tiles.

The hills conquered, the engineer could relax and take his line along a level route. Emerging, as it were, back into the light, the walker is faced by a splendid vista of rolling chalkland and what appear to be a number of basking whales on the horizon. These whale-like lumps are in fact barrows, Bronze Age burial mounds – reminders that the railwaymen were very much Johnny-come-latelys in this landscpe. One might expect that the line might now prove difficult to follow, but it remains, in fact, perfectly distinct, a broad stony track between the fields. This stoniness, a result of years of ballasting to bed down the sleepers, perhaps explains why no-one has thought it worth while to plough over the route. This is very much horse country, and not your commonplace hack either. Carefully maintained and well laid out runs, many with hurdles, show that this is thoroughbred country. It is not perhaps quite so thickly populated by equine inhabitants as nearby Lambourn, but this is racehorse territory nevertheless.

The deep cutting and the slanting bridge proclaim this to be an abandoned railway. It is, in fact, part of the Didcot, Newbury and Southampton Junction Railway. But already, trees are growing in the track bed, as nature reclaims the ground.

By the time Compton is reached, the route has provided some excellent scenery, and also fine examples of the range of techniques used by railway engineers in the nineteenth century. It has also provided numerous problems of access, with several sections closed off by barbed wire fences – not to mention the more serious deterrent to walkers in the shape of the rifle range. Eight thousand miles of abandoned railway there may be, but public access is decidedly limited. It is possible to gain access by chasing up the local authorities, land owners, and so on – and, of course, by trespassing which, needless to say, is an activity which the author would not dream of recommending to anyone! Often it seems, the use of old railways is denied to walkers and others for no better reason than that the British have always been fonder of keeping people out of places than they have been of letting them in. Fortunately, this is not universally so and, in the latter half of the book, twenty-one specific walks will be described in detail and a list given of very many more where the local authorities have taken over lines specifically to open them up for the public enjoyment.

As well as demonstrating some of the problems and delights of walking the line, my 8-mile stroll from Didcot to Compton also emphasized, for me at any rate, just how far my pleasure was enhanced by knowing something of the history of the line. In fact, I found I wanted to know a good deal more and, as soon as I reached home, I began thumbing through reference books. The line proved to have had an interesting history, if not one that was exactly covered with glory. The Didcot, Newbury and Southampton Junction Railway began life in 1882 and was intended to provide a north-south link between the Great Western at Didcot and the London and South Western in Hampshire, from whence passengers could continue to Southampton. But, as with many small companies, begun with modest and sensible proposals, the D.N.S.J.R. grew more ambitious. They could, they decided, dispense with the L.S.W.R. altogether and make their own, independent way to Southampton. It was not a good idea. They made it as far as Winchester and there they stuck: the cash had run out. Cap in hand, the directors called on the London and South Western saying, 'Please, sir, may we use your lines to Southampton?'. Permission was given, but on the L.S.W.R.'s terms. The line now had a role to play, but not quite the star part that the promoters had dreamed of when work began.

The line was never a great success, though it was given something of a new lease of life when it was absorbed into the Great Western empire. Does any of this make any difference to the walker? I believe it does, for most of us who walk the line have somewhere in our minds images of the railway as it was in its working days. Seeing the magical initials G.W.R., we might dream of great main line expresses thundering through, long trains of coaches in the famous brown and cream livery strung out behind them. Reality was rather different. The service was, to put it at its kindliest, intermittent. True, the line had its days of glory during World War II when the status of the route was greatly enhanced by the doubling of the track. On the whole, however, it was a quiet and somewhat unsuccessful branch line that never rose to the heights for which it was intended. But it did run, and there are railwaymen around who remember its running. Life on these little-used routes was certainly different from that of the main lines. One fireman – who must certainly remain anonymous – recalled how they used to slow down to a crawl at one section so that he could lob a few shovelsful of coal into a certain trackside back garden. It is always worth remembering that, though the railway is now dead, it was once very much alive.

It is, I believe, true to say that the more you know about railways, the more interesting a walk along the tracks becomes. That is not to say that those who know nothing about the subject can obtain no pleasure at all from a railway walk – far from it. Old railways provide uniquely fascinating routes through both town and country, but they remain man-made, artificial routes. Almost inevitably, one finds questions coming to mind – why does the line go this way rather than that? who travelled this route and why? and what sort of machines were in use? The more you think you know, the more the questions multiply and the more fascinating the whole exercise becomes – and I use the word 'exercise' deliberately for, if railway walking does nothing else, it does get us out of the dusty archives and into the open air.

Even our one short stretch of line has thrown up all kinds of intriguing questions. Yet this is a comparatively late line, built at the end of the first great age of main line construction. When did the railway age itself begin? The answer to that question depends very much on how you define your terms. Most of us think of railways as a system laid out with iron or steel rails along which locomotives haul goods and passengers. This is certainly a description of the Didcot, Newbury and Southampton Junction Railway we have just been looking at. But the *Oxford English Dictionary* has a different definition. It describes it as 'a way or road laid with rails on which the wheels of wagons containing heavy goods are made to run for ease of transport'. It is only in a secondary definition that any mention is made of locomotive engines. I prefer the first definition. It is quite true that the railway system we travel today was originally built to take the steam locomotive and, in our railway walks, we shall find many reminders of the age of steam. We shall, however, see far more evidence of the thinking of the civil engineers who designed the route than we shall of the mechanical engineers who built the machines. And the civil engineering of railways dates back far beyond the invention of the steam locomotive. There were railways in Britain for more than two centuries before the opening of the Stockton and Darlington Railway in 1825. If these earlier lines had not existed, then the rail system of Britain might well have developed in quite different directions. They did exist, their tracks can be followed, and, if they are by no means such obvious features in the landscape as the more familiar railways, then they do at least provide scope for some interesting detective work. It is with these modest predecessors of the great Victorian railway age that our historic survey begins.

A memento of the railway past: this plaque is fastened to the wall of the cottage where George Stephenson was born. It stands beside the Wylam Tramway, and so encompasses both the tramway and the railway age: it would not be too fanciful to say that it was here that the true railway age began.

2 HORSE POWER – THE TRAMWAY AGE

God bless the man wi' peace and plenty
That first invented metal plates.
Draw out his years to five times twenty
Then slide him through the heavenly gates.

This would appear to be the first recorded example of a poem written in praise of a railway engineer. It was penned by Thomas Wilson and the verses refer to John Curr who first introduced metal rails into collieries in 1776, thereby saving the miners the terrible labour of hauling out the coal on their own backs. To get the full flavour of the lines you need to read them in a Geordie accent, for it was in the north-east of England that the lines were written and the great event occurred. It was here, too, that much of the early railway development was concentrated, in the collieries of Durham and Northumberland. But, if one tries to turn back to the true origins of railways to discover just when people first hit on the notion of using rails to ease the movement of wheeled carriages, then you have to look back far beyond the eighteenth century.

It was generally recognized, at a very early date, that laying down some sort of track was a good idea, but the first tracks of all reversed the general railway principle. Wheels moved in ruts rather than on rails or raised track, and what is thought to be an example of a Roman road of this type can be seen on Blackstone Edge in Lancashire. So, if you take your definition of a railway as being a route where wheeled traffic moves on a fixed track, then you could start your railway walks by making your way up to Rishworth Moor to the east of Littleborough. Not many of us, however, would accept that as a railway and there is, in any case, some doubt about the significance of the grooves and even about the date of the track. So when did railways first come to Britain?

Although Britain pioneered the great railway age, the first rails were probably laid in Germany some time in the middle of the sixteenth century. They were wooden rails, used in mines, and similar tracks were soon being laid in British mines as well. No original wooden rails have survived on the surface, but occasionally lengths can be found in situ in long-abandoned underground workings. I have come across examples as far apart as Derbyshire and the Forest of Dean. By the end of the sixteenth century, wooden rails known as 'tilting rails' were being laid at British collieries to take vehicles with flanged wheels. Something that is very recognizably a railway had arrived.

The earliest railways for which we have definite records were short lines joining collieries to rivers, from Broseley in Shropshire to the Severn, and from Wollaton in Nottingham to the Trent. Navigable rivers then formed the major trading routes of Britain, so that anything which eased the movement between colliery and

river was of great utility. These early railways consisted of wooden cross sleepers, familiar with later railways, and wooden rails on which waggons with flanged wheels could be run. Indeed, if you substituted metal rails for wood then you had a perfectly conventional modern rail system. Most of these early lines were built with a slight but steady gradient down towards the river, so that loaded waggons could descend under gravity and the empty waggons could then be pulled back by horses. Early illustrations show coal waggons with the 'train driver' perched on the back of the waggon with a vast lever operating the brakes close to hand, while the horse trots behind. In some cases, the horse's energy was conserved and it was provided with its very own waggon so that it could ride in style down the hill.

Waggon ways such as this seldom involved any great construction problems: but there were exceptions. In the 1720s, the builders of the line from Tanfield in County Durham found themselves confronted with the Houghwell Burn which ran in a deep valley right across their proposed route. They decided to bridge the gap with a single arch – a bold decision, for no arch of comparable size existed anywhere in Britain. The job was handed over to a local mason, who completed his task in 1726. The stone bridge is still a mightily impressive structure, crossing the ravine in a 103-foot (31.3-metre) span. Variously known as the Tanfield or Causey Arch, it carries the distinction of being the oldest railway bridge in the world and, where many 'firsts', are but poor shadows of the

How many of those boating on the Avon at Stratford or walking over this flat-topped bridge realize that it is a survivor from the days of the tramways, and once carried the Stratford and Moreton Railway?

mightier works that are to come, this elegant bridge will stand comparison with the best. It is, in fact, as good a place as any to begin an exploration of early railways, and is to be found just off the A6076 between Stanley and Sunniside (OS map reference NZ 2056). The setting is superb with the arch rising in its splendour above a thickly wooded gorge – and it is considerably easier to see now than it was a few years ago, for the authorities have cut back the trees and built a viewing platform. This is a great boon to photographers – I well recall my own first visit in the early seventies when, after much scrambling up and down the steep banks, it eventually became clear that the only picture that would be obtained would be taken standing directly beneath the arch. Another recent innovation at the site is the laying of a short length of wooden rail on which sits a replica waggon or chaldron, of the type that would have run here when the line first opened. There are other reasons, too, for visiting the spot, for the line of the old route which carried a double 4-foot (1.2-metre) gauge track can be traced round on an embankment to the main section of the waggonway. This was later taken over by the North Eastern Railway. Here you will find Marley Hill Station, now home to the Tanfield Railway, a preserved steam line which, at the time of writing, is open to visitors every Sunday, with locomotives in steam throughout the summer months. Nowhere else can you see such a pattern of railway use that extends back for more than two-and-a-half centuries. This is by no means the end of the story. Nearby is the splendid North of England Open Air Museum at Beamish Hall, which includes among its exhibits a colliery restoration, the centre piece of which is the Beamish steam winding engine. This is essentially a nineteenth-century scene but, on the railway track outside, are lined up rows of chaldrons, descendants of the wooden waggons that ran over the Causey Arch. The site is something of a Mecca for steam and railway enthusiasts for, on these tracks, the replica of Stephenson's *Locomotion No. 1* is regularly steamed. But we are now leaping too far forward in time, to the steam locomotive age. In the area round Causey Arch, it is not always easy to separate out the different layers of railway history.

Scotland's first waggonway was born out of war, and was to see war again soon after its opening – and can probably claim to be the only railway in Britain over which land forces have waged war. The line is the Tranent-Cockenzie waggonway which, like its southern equivalents was built to join a colliery to water transport, the colliery being at Tranent and the water being the port of Cockenzie and Port Seton on the coast to the east of Edinburgh. After the unsuccessful rising of 1715, many Scottish nobles found their property forfeit to the crown and, among them, was the Earl of Winton. His Tranent colliery was sold off to a London company that built the waggonway. In 1745, the Scots rose again and the Young Pretender took Edinburgh. General Sir John Cope set up his forces along the waggonway near Prestonpans, using a low embankment as cover for cannon and men. Charles Stuart attacked in the early morning taking the government troops by surprise, and the Battle of Prestonpans was soon over. The section

A reconstruction of an early chaldron or coal waggon on display beside the Causey Arch. This early railway vehicle is notable for the solid wooden wheels and the massive hand brake.

where the battle was fought is easily traced from the stone marker at the junction of the A198 and the B6371. Tranent itself is now home to the Prestongrange Mining Museum where a fine beam pumping engine of 1874 is preserved. Although the track bed of this historic line is clearly distinguishable for much of its length, there are few features of any great significance to be seen. Rather more interesting from this point of view is the slightly later line built further north in Alloa, which joined a local colliery to a glass works. The line passed right through the town centre, where two short tunnels have survived.

Apart from the already mentioned underground survivors, the replica track at Tanfield and a few examples in museums, it is very rare to have an opportunity to see any physical track remains from the waggonway age. The wood rots and was never very long lasting, even when in use. Wear and tear of the wooden rails were major problems. It was soon realized that rail life could be extended by laying a metal strip along the top, providing protection just as the iron tyre protected the wooden cart wheel. The great change came when the wooden rail was dispensed with altogether, and the waggonway gave way to the plateway and tramway. This happened during the canal age and, in this period of their history, rivers, canals, and railways were all intimately connected.

The first metal rails were cast iron, manufactured at the famous Abraham Darby works at Coalbrookdale. There is probably no other concern that had such an impact on world industrial history as this. Here iron was first smelted using coke, the first iron bridge was constructed, and parts for early steam engines were cast as well as the rails. These were not, however, rails as we know them today. They were L-shaped in section, designed to take trucks with plain wheels instead of the flanged wheels used with wooden rails as well as on modern rail systems. Coalbrookdale remains one of the few places where such track remains in situ. It can be seen, for example, leading out of the old Gothic iron warehouse beside the Severn in Ironbridge, along the wharf to the river. In the same area, you can also see a specialized use of iron rails as an adjunct to canal transport: the inclined plane. The Shropshire tub-boat canal runs through the Blists Hill open air museum site, high above the Severn. Connection by water was clearly impossible, so a system was built whereby the tubs could be floated on to wheeled bogies on a railed track that ran down the slope to the Coalport Canal beside the Severn, where the tubs could be floated off again. In the typical inclined plane, the tracks were doubled and tubs counterbalanced so that, as loaded tubs descended the slope, the empties were hauled back up again. Very little, if any, power was required, and such systems are known as self-acting inclines. A number of such tub-boat canals were built the most extensive being the Bude Canal in Cornwall. A far more common solution to the problem of making connections with canals in hilly country, however, was to dispense with the tub-boat and trans-ship the cargo between canal boat and horse-drawn waggon. Such routes became known as tramways or plateways.

The first connections of this type date back to the wooden rail age, and the construction of the Caldon Canal, an extension of the Trent and Mersey Canal, completed in 1779. It is an extraordinarily beautiful canal which ends at Froghall Basin, but it was built to connect the Potteries with the limestone quarries at Caldon Low which, paradoxically, stands some 700 feet (213 metres) higher up in the hills. Tramways were the obvious answer and, over the years, a number of such connections was made. Today, Froghall Basin is a picnic area with industrial overtones, in the form of an impressive range of lime kilns, above which the old routes can be easily traced leading off towards the quarries. A similar system on an even grander scale can be seen at the end of the Peak Forest Canal at Buxworth – a gentrified form of older Bugsworth – Basin. This is, in many ways, far more typical of the tramway age, for the engineer responsible for much of the work was Benjamin Outram, a name so closely associated with the development of these early railways that many have claimed, quite erroneously, that the very name 'tramway' was derived from Outram. The whole canal is liberally supplied with rail connections and, at Whaley Bridge, there is a unique canal-rail interchange. The Peak Forest Canal ends here at a point where a large stone building has been constructed over the water. The tramway emerges from the opposite end of the same building, heading off towards Buxton and Cromford (*see* page 62).

It was Outram as much as anyone who was responsible for establishing the form of the tramways. His lines were constructed using short lengths of rail, held in place by spikes driven into square, stone sleeper blocks. Old wooden rails have rotted and decayed, iron rails have been lifted and sent for scrap, but the stone sleeper blocks have proved more durable and today provide solid evidence for those in search of old lines that they are indeed on the right track. And the canal system remains the best starting place in the hunt for tramways. They can be found extending the lengths of many canals – the Ashby and the Macclesfield being outstanding examples. But if one had to choose just one region to travel in the hunt for tramways, then it would have to be among the hills and valleys of South Wales.

The Brecon and Abergavenny Canal was begun with the authorization of an Act of Parliament of 1793, which allowed for 'making and maintaining a navigable Canal from the town of Brecknock to the Monmouthshire Canal, near the town of Pontypool, in the county of Monmouth; and for making and maintaining Railways and Stone Roads to several Iron Works and Mines'. This was a time when railways were not considered of sufficient importance to warrant an Act all to themselves. There were, in fact, fourteen separate tramways connecting with the canal and, as some of these also connected with tramways of the nearby Monmouth Canal, they form an intricate network joining ironworks, mines, and quarries to the waterway system. Tracing these routes often involves a strong detective instinct, for their tracks are nowhere near as plain as those of the later railway age. In fact, one is often quite unsure about being on the right route, until some reassuring piece of physical evidence is spotted. But, if walking tramways is more complicated than walking conventional

railways, it does have its own rewards as the tramways of the Brecon and Abergavenny Canal amply demonstrate. Not least among those rewards is the magnificent hill scenery.

My own first excursions began some years ago, but I had the opportunity for a more thorough investigation during a canal holiday in the summer of 1982. My first walk was along the Brinore tramway which joins the canal near Talybont. It was built from newly established iron works at Rhymney, one of the many new towns established at the heads of the steep valleys that run north to south in this part of the country. But where exactly is the tramway and how do you find it? That is not such an easy question to answer. The starting point is a row of lime kilns on the canal bank to the east of the lift bridge. A route appears as a track beside hedgerows and soon begins climbing off to the south through a conifer plantation, and it is at this point that doubts begin to creep in. Can any railway ever have climbed so steeply? Just when you are quite certain you have taken a wrong turning, you look at the path beneath your feet and there they are, the old stone sleeper blocks with the spike holes in the centre. There is an immense feeling of satisfaction in knowing that, in spite of all appearances to the contrary, you are on track after all. It is possible to continue over the top to Rhymney or to follow another, equally attractive route to the quarries at Trefil. Trefil does, in fact, provide an

Llanfoist on the beautiful Brecon and Abergavenny Canal was once one of the busiest spots on the waterway. Trucks laden with iron came down the hillside on the tramway incline to unload in the warehouse. Canal boats could then be floated in beneath the building for transhipment.

alternative access point for those travelling by road rather than by water because it can be reached by a minor road off the A465 just north of Tredegar. As a bonus, there is a view of the later and very fine Trefil viaduct. There is also, for lovers of curiosities, a marked stone near the quarries called 'The Duke's Stone'. Having always assumed that this had some immensely romantic association, I was more than a little disappointed to discover that it marked nothing more exotic than the spot at which the Duke of Beaufort had a picnic while out shooting grouse.

The Brinore tramway offers a good introduction to tramways and the Brecon hills but, best of all the routes, both for its magnificent scenery and the fascinating details met along the way, is Hill's tramway which runs from Llanfoist to Blaenavon. It offers a walk which would be a delight to anyone who enjoys hill scenery but, for the tramway detective or industrial historian, it offers a veritable feast.

The canal at this point takes a high-level route around the heavily wooded flank of the tall hill, Blorenge, and here at least the start of the tramway is easily identified. The narrow, steep road up from the village ends in a bridge – a flat-topped bridge, not the familiar hump back usually found straddling canals. This is, in fact, the tramway bridge itself and, crossing it, you at once find yourself confronted with a fascinating group of buildings and structures. The canal at this point widens out into a basin with wharf, wharf manager's house, and warehouse. This warehouse is built up against the embankment on the shoulder of the hill, so that trucks coming down the wharf could unload directly in at first-floor level. The ground floor is open to the canal, so that boats could be floated in beneath the trucks and loaded directly through trap doors in the floor of the upper storey: time and motion studies were not, perhaps, a twentieth-century invention after all. The building is known as the iron warehouse and iron pigs in a preserved truck outside show where it derived its name and what was the main trade of tramway and canal. The wharf manager's house looks out over the waterway and also upwards to the steep track leading through the woods. This was the route of the tramway – straight up this almost precipitous slope. There is one other feature of note at Llanfoist, the tunnel beneath the canal. Without that, pedestrians would have been forced to cross the water via the tramway bridge, sharing their journey with the busy movement of trucks. This was not necessarily a good idea for tramways were by no means the safest or the most reliable form of transport. The Duke of Rutland came here in 1805 and described the situation as he found it, with waggons hurtling down the slope:

Indeed they acquire so great a degree of velocity in their descent, that a man is forced to walk or run behind the cart, with a kind of rudder or pole affixed to the hind-wheel, which he locks up when it proceeds too fast. Should this pole break (which it sometimes does) the waggon flies away, and overturns everything it meets. . . . Last year, Mr. Frere, the proprietor of the iron works, was returning from London, and going along the rail-road in a post-chaise, when about a hundred yards from him, he saw one of those waggons coming down upon him, with astonishing velocity. He could not possibly get out of the way, and must have been crushed to pieces, if fortunately the waggon had not broken over the iron groove, which had hitherto kept it in the track, and run forcibly up an ash-tree by the side of the road, in the branches of which it literally stuck, and thus saved him from immediate destruction.

Luckily for those setting off along the track today, they have nothing worse to fear than an uphill slog and, in summer, a remarkably active insect population. Once again, the route seems impossible, and only the presence of numerous stone sleeper blocks provides reassurance that all is well and the walker is indeed following the correct route. The incline is in three sections, not quite in line, separated by small platforms where the winding drums for hauling up the incline and controlling the descent of the laden trucks had been fixed. By the time you emerge from the woods at the top of the slope you are more than 750 feet (228 metres) above the level of the canal and can look forward to some easier walking. The tramway now follows the contour round the western side of the hill and, instead of the dark, insect-ridden woods, you have grass and bracken and a splendid view across the valley of the Usk to the Brecon Beacons. The route is now

The oldest surviving railway bridge in the world, the Causey Arch reaches across the Houghwell Burn in a single stride, and seems as solidly elegant now as when it was built two-and-a-half centuries ago.

somewhat more difficult to follow though it is roughly coincident with the pathway shown on the ordnance survey map. There is at least one feature of note, a short tunnel at SO 272 129 and the line eventually reaches the B4246 at SO 256 122. From here it could scarcely be plainer for it appears as a broad shelf, swinging away to the quarries of Pwll-Du. And here, alas, the route ends for the walker for, just beyond the old Pwll-Du village hall, the tramway disappears into the long tunnel that led all the way down to Blaenavon – and, at Blaenavon itself, the marks of the tramway have long been obliterated. It is, however, well worth visiting Blaenavon for otherwise the tramway makes no sort of sense at all – it is in the town that all becomes clear. Here is the best-preserved example of an early iron-making site to be found anywhere in Britain, the vast stone towers of the blast furnaces rearing up from the hillside like ramparts. Across the valley can be seen the prominent head gear of the Big Pit colliery, now an important mining museum. This whole area was developed around coal and iron, with the transport needs supplied by canal and tramway. The canals were limited to the valleys, with the tramways providing the ways across the hills. The Brecon and Abergavenny Canal and its connection provide outstanding examples set in outstanding scenery.

There are, however, many other impressive remains of the tramway age in South Wales. At Hirwaun, the remains of the blast furnaces – less impressive than those of Blaenavon, but impressive enough – can be seen set against the hillside. Above them, the tramway sweeps round on a high embankment on top of which the lines of sleeper blocks appear with remarkable clarity. Not far away in Robertstown to the north of Aberdare is a bridge which scores a first to put beside that of the Causey Arch, for here the Llwydcoed tramway of 1811 is carried across the river on an iron bridge, the first of its kind on any railway. Such sites may not always be part of long, interesting walks, but they do help to make the point that it was on these early routes that the expertise was developed which was to be used in the railways of the nineteenth century.

Not all tramways were thought of as adjuncts to canals – by the end of the eighteenth century they were being considered as alternatives. The engineer William Jessop, the man responsible for such major canal schemes as the Grand Junction, now the Grand Union, Canal was asked to advise on a proposed canal from the Thames at Wandsworth along the Wandle Valley to Croydon. He reported in 1799 that the canal was impractical but that there was '. . . another way of obtaining the object in view; if not quite as effectually as by a Canal, it will, under all circumstances, be not much inferior to it; this is by the adoption of an Iron Railway'. Work began on the Surrey Iron Railway in 1801, the first of its kind in southern England and also, more importantly, the first public goods railway to be approved by Act of Parliament. Before then, railways and tramways had been purely the concern of industrialists; now here was a railway in the capital city itself and available as a general carrier of goods. Not much now remains, though the line of an extension can be traced running off the A237

towards Mitcham Station, and still called Tramway Path, while the builders of a nearby housing estate have also spotted the connection and named it Jessop Place. There is, however, one other spot, where there are physical remains of the line – Young's brewery at Wandsworth. There are many reasons for visiting the brewery – apart from the excellent ale. They still have a pair of beam engines at work; they still stable dray horses; and they have something like a small farmyard out the back where wanders a real, live version of the Young's emblem, a ram. They also have part of the Surrey Iron Railway, for stone sleeper blocks can be seen incorporated in the brewery wall.

The Surrey line was the first of a number of similar routes built much as the later railways were built – as public carriers – but designed for horse-drawn not steam-drawn trains. One outstanding survivor from this age is the bridge built to carry the Stratford and Moreton Railway across the Avon at Stratford. The nine-arched viaduct is a handsome structure, and its flat deck would have

The line of Hill's Tramway is unmistakable, a flat ledge carved into the hillside. This section is curving away towards the quarries at Pwll-Du.

provided a clue to its railway origins – even without the preserved waggon and restored section of rail at the town end. The line was completed in 1826, which makes it more or less a contemporary of the Stockton and Darlington, so the old bridge might be thought of as not just a link between the two banks of the Avon but also as spanning the age of the horse tramway and the steam railway. Yet there are, in fact, other lines with rather more of a claim to that distinction than the Stratford tramway.

The first and most obvious candidate is the Penydarren tramway, described in more detail on pages 58–61, where Trevithick made his first successful experiments to run a steam locomotive on iron rails. The second candidate is the Middleton Colliery Railway on the edge of Leeds. This, too, was begun as a horse-drawn line, taking coal from the pit to the Aire and Calder Navigation. But then, when the Napoleonic Wars sent the price of fodder sky-high, the colliery manager, John Blenkinsop, decided to try to replace his horses with steam engines. He was well aware that earlier trials had been unsuccessful largely because the heavy locomotives had broken up the brittle cast-iron rails, so he decided to use light locomotives and secure the necessary traction and drawing power by adding an extra, toothed wheel to the locomotive which would engage with a third, toothed rail. In other words, he introduced a rack and pinion system. It worked – and Britain's first successful commercial steam railway was on its way, and in this century it became the first standard gauge railway to be run by enthusiasts as a preserved line. Nothing remains of the Blenkinsop system, nor indeed of any of the original tramway, but a road above the site is called Old Run Road. It follows part of the original route, and stone sleeper blocks can still be seen incorporated into the wall beside the road.

My final site to take us out of the tramway age and on to the new age is, in many ways, the most significant of them all. It can be found among the collieries of the north-east where so many early developments were to be seen. The Wylam Waggonway was typical of the region, but the colliery that it served was a progressive concern – the only one in the area to order one of the new-fangled steam locomotives from Richard Trevithick following the successful trial at Penydarren. Alas, it was a failure and suffered the ignominy of being removed from its wheels for use as a stationary engine. Horses continued in use just as they had in June 1781 when a local collier's wife gave birth to a son in a cottage beside the tracks. The family name was Stephenson, and the little boy was called George. The line itself has changed many times, becoming adapted eventually as a branch line of the North Eastern Railway and continuing in use until the 1960s. Now it is closed and you can walk the line and call in at the cottage, now owned by the National Trust. One room has been refurnished in nineteenth-century style and, from it, you can look out over the line young George Stephenson watched. For him, the steam engine lay in the future, was yet to appear chugging past the cottage door. For us, it is largely a thing of the past, preserved in museums or run thanks to the efforts of volunteers. But here at Wylam the two ages of the railway meet.

THE GOLDEN AGE OF STEAM

3

The early waggonways and tramways have a great deal to offer to the walker. Unlike their successors of the steam age, they were not constrained by the need to maintain a more-or-less level course, but could cheerfully charge up hillsides and swoop down to the valleys. They can often be found and traced in remote and beautiful countryside and, among the tracts that can be walked and studied, are some of unique importance in railway history. They can, however, tax the ingenuity of those who would follow their routes, for a good deal of detective work is often required if the lines are to be located at all, let alone followed throughout their lengths. The later railways rarely suffer from this disadvantage, if it is considered a disadvantage rather than a challenge. The routes are usually plain enough and easy to follow, though there may be problems of access. They do, however, suffer in comparison with their predecessors in one important respect: the lines available for walking are rarely lines of the first importance. The great trunk routes of the nineteenth century are mostly still in use today, so the walker is usually relegated to the branch lines and light railways felled by the Beeching axe. This is not altogether true, for there is at least one crucial exception: the line thought of by many as marking the beginning of the modern age, the Stockton and Darlington Railway.

It was by no means immediately obvious that the line was to have any special significance. When the first Act of Parliament authorizing construction was passed in 1821, it described the line as 'a Railway or Tramway, from the River Tees, at Stockton to Wilton Park Colliery, with several Branches therefrom'. It was, in short, just another tramway to be constructed of metal plates on stone blocks joining a colliery to a river. Then George Stephenson arrived on the scene and, in a historic meeting with one of the Company's directors, Edward Pearse, persuaded the latter to change from a plateway to an edge railway – the railway of the type we know today with flanged wheels running over the rails – and, more importantly, to aim from the first at using steam locomotives for haulage. There was much argument, but the Stephenson-Pearse group won the day and the engineer who had originally been appointed to build the line went back to his home in Wales. Ironically, the unsuccessful gentleman was George Overton, engineer of the Penydarren tramway where Trevithick's first successful experiments with the steam locomotive had taken place. Stephenson was now put in charge of building the line, and a new route was set out which required a new Act of Parliament. The new Act had one important difference from the old: it specifically mentioned steam engines – stationary engines for cable haulage and locomotives. For the first time in the world, a public railway was to be built specifically intended for use by steam locomotives. It was not, however, to be given over exclusively to the new engines. Locomotives were, at first, limited to hauling coal: passengers travelled in a horse-drawn coach, a conventional stage coach mounted on flanged wheels. One can imagine the chaos this mixed traffic must have caused. It was not, in any case, a particularly busy passenger line. An old poster for the 'Experiment' as the S. & D.R. coach-on-rails was called, advertises a morning coach leaving Stockton at 7.30 and reaching Darlington 'about half-past nine' with a return trip starting at 3 pm. It was a modest start, but it proved the worth of the steam locomotive and of Stephenson the engineer – and it was to lead on to greater things.

Much of the original route is still in use today, but there is one place where the local authorities have marked out a railway walk which gives something of the feel of this important line. The route officially starts at Shildon, but there is a great deal to be said for starting at the far end of the walk for, in this way, the route unfolds in a developing historical perspective from tramway to fully fledged railway. The route then begins at Phoenix Row (NZ 167292) an area once liberally supplied with collieries – and, in fact, the reason that nothing of the line can be traced north of here is its obliteration by mining. From a bend in the road, the line runs south on a high embankment to the two Etherley inclines, not very dramatic slopes but sufficiently steep for the company to build a steam engine at the top so that the trucks could be hauled up by cable. A few scattered stones are all that now remain of the engine house. In fact, this section of the line went out of use as early as the 1840s with the completion of the Wear Valley line.

The line continued on to West Auckland where it crossed the River Gaunless on a cast iron bridge. The bridge has gone, but has not been lost, for it is preserved at the National Railway Museum at York. This is still the heart of the busy mining area that called the S. & D.R. into being and, just beyond, is the impressive Brusselton incline. Here can be seen many of the old stone sleeper blocks still in place while the cottage at the top incorporates the engine house for winding up the incline. Throughout this section it is quite obvious that what we are seeing is the traditional pattern of colliery railway-cum-plateway with its level sections used for horse-drawn traffic and inclines with steam-powered cable hauling between. It represents, in fact, not so much the start of a new age as the end of an old. It is only when we reach Shildon itself that we find the signs that the S. & D.R. is something more than another relic from tramway days. The line runs along the side of the British Rail Shildon works, once the pride of the region but sadly sentenced to death in 1983. Here one joins the working railway and, at the level crossing at the Mason's Arms, is the first of the sites which have helped to make this stretch of line world famous. It was here on Tuesday 27 September 1825 that the engine *Locomotion* was attached to its train for the opening ceremony or, as the official invitation had it, 'A superior locomotive, of the most superior construction, will be employed with a train of convenient carriages, for the conveyance of the proprietors and strangers'.

The proprietors and strangers had to make the most of this brief flirtation with the wonders of steam for, after the opening, they had to be content with the horse-drawn *Experiment*. In Shildon, there was also a privately operated passenger service which worked on the main line, and a short colliery branch line, the Surtees Railway. The old coach house run by Daniel Adamson can be seen on the corner of Main Street and Byerley Road. But we are soon back with strong memories of the steam age when we walk along Soho Street to the north of the railroad to the site of the Soho engine works.

On that famous day in 1825 when *Locomotion* had made the first run, the footplate had been manned by George Stephenson and his brother James, while the guard had been Timothy Hackworth, resident engineer of the S. & D.R. Shildon was Hackworth's headquarters though, when he first came to the site, it was described as 'a wet swampy field – a likely place to find a snipe or a flock of peewits'. Here houses were built and a row of original cottages still survives, together with Hackworth's own house which is now a museum. More importantly, workshops were built for the repair and maintenance of the engines and rolling stock, while Hackworth later established his own locomotive works. Just one building of Hackworth's Soho Works survives, the old paint shop, and that is now home to an exhibit that takes us on to the next, and perhaps the decisive stage, in the transition to the steam age. The exhibit is a working replica of Hackworth's locomotive, the *Sans Pareil*, built to take part in the Rainhill Trial of 1829. These tests were set up by the Liverpool and Manchester Railway to see which, if any, design of engine would be suitable for all haulage, passenger and goods, on their new line. It was, of course, Stephenson's *Rocket* that carried the day, but the hopes of Shildon rode with the Hackworth engine. It was very much an S. & D.R. design, and there were many who claimed it should have won the prize – fate was to prove kinder to the replica than it had been to the original.

I well remember the day in November 1979 when a small group of us stood around watching the boiler pressure slowly mount up as *Sans Pareil* number two prepared for the first run. It was a triumphant success and the engineer in charge, Colin Umpleby, was almost as ecstatic as Jane Hackworth Young, a direct descendant of the original engineer. There was very much a feeling in the air that Shildon pride was to be put to the test again when Rainhill was rerun. Replicas of the contenders were due to appear before the crowds: *Novelty* never started successfully, and *Rocket*, the star of the show, was sadly derailed, leaving steady, solid *Sans Pareil* to carry the day. There were some very cheery faces – and some distinctly slurred north-eastern accents – in our hotel that night.

Sans Pareil, Rocket, and Rainhill take us right into the Golden Age. Henceforth, when people spoke of railways, they would be talking about routes designed for general carrying where haulage would be by steam locomotive. The Liverpool and Manchester was soon followed by another main line route, the London and Birmingham, and then a flood of new routes was suddenly appearing in the form of prospectuses if not always in the shape of tracks on the ground. The years of the railway mania had arrived. Among the many new routes successfully promoted, there were some necessarily doomed to failure, planned to run over impossible ground to link unlikely termini. Others were highly successful, none more so than Brunel's Great Western. Stephenson had set his rails 4 feet 8½ inches (1.43 metres) apart, for no better reason than that was the gauge in use at the local colliery. Brunel argued that rails set 7 feet (2.13 metres) apart would provide a better, more efficient, and faster ride, so the broad gauge tracks were duly laid. Standard gauge and broad gauge co-existed right through to 1892, when the battle of the gauges was decided with Stephenson's standard emerging victorious. But the argument over which was the better system has never quite faded away.

These were the years which set the pattern for the railway system we know today. It was then that the major engineering ideas were worked out – so that, when we walk an old railway line today, we are seeing the physical evidence of those ideas first established a century-and-a-half ago. As originally planned, the L. & M.R. followed the pattern of earlier lines, with level sections alternating with inclines on which cable haulage was to be used. The inclines were, in the main, very gentle affairs with gradients little more than 1 in 100. These were to prove no obstacle to *Rocket* and its successors, and very soon the inclined plane was all but eliminated from the railway engineer's vocabulary. Lines were to be built that could be worked by locomotives throughout their length. This meant that such routes needed to be kept level or at best a moderate gradient might be allowed – 1 in 100 was generally considered to mark the limits of acceptability. Main lines were, however, built later with more extravagant gradients in the hills,

The replica of Timothy Hackworth's locomotive, *Sans Pareil*, being returned to the shed at Shildon after an excursion under its own steam. The original of this engine was the pride of the Stockton and Darlington Railway when it was entered for the Rainhill Trial of 1825.

and the Highland Railway engineers of the 1850s were forced to construct a line with a ruling gradient of 1 in 70. Yet even this was modest compared with the old tramway inclines, not to mention the steep slopes that could easily be accepted on the roads. To keep to these limits involved some spectacular engineering works.

The technique principally used was that known as 'cut and fill', pioneered by the canal engineers but perfected on the railways. It consisted of cutting through rising ground and then using the excavated material to build up embankments across the next valley. It is possible to make a direct comparison of the two generations of construction by visiting Tring in the Chilterns. Here, side by side, are William Jessop's Grand Union Canal and Robert Stephenson's London and Birmingham Railway. Both pierce the hills in deep cuttings but, when they emerge on the northern side, the canal engineer was able to overcome the difference in levels by twisting and turning down the hill and by building a series of locks. Stephenson carried right on with a long embankment. There was, however, one other factor which drew the two generations together – the work force.

Canals and railways mostly used the same unsophisticated methods. The engineer would determine the route and the construction techniques to be used, but the actual job of building was let out to independent contractors. They, in their turn, employed a small army of itinerant workers, the navvies, the name being an abbreviation of 'navigators', the men who dug the canal navigations. When walking the line today, it is worth remembering that everything was built with muscle power – no great, earth-moving machines, just men with picks, shovels, and barrows. As you walk down one of the deep cuttings that you will find on almost every railway walk, just imagine the effort that went into digging them out. Have a go at walking up the steep sides – and then stretch your imagination as well as your legs and try to conceive how you would set about pushing a barrow load of clay and rock up the same slope. It seems impossible, and would have been impossible without the barrow runs. Planks were laid up the side of the cutting and a rope let down, one end of which was fastened to the barrow and then tied round the navvy's waist. At the top, the rope was attached to a horse. When everything was ready, the horse was set on a steady walk while the barrow and navvy were hauled slowly up the bank. At the top, the barrow was emptied and the navvy returned down the plank, pulling the barrow behind him. It was arduous work, and dangerous, for if the horse faltered or the man slipped on the greasy plank, barrow and contents could all but bury the navvy. In the great Tring cutting where there were more than twenty runs, injuries were common-place and one man was killed. Some cuttings, however, had to be made through solid rock – the deep Olive Mount cutting on the Liverpool and Manchester Railway being a notable example – and here the engineers had to blast their way through with black powder. The smooth, level path the walker follows was only achieved through much sweat and too much blood.

Cut and fill alone was never enough to cope with the larger lumps and deeper hollows of the British landscape, which called for more drastic measures – viaducts and tunnels. Both are to be seen on what is scenically one of the most spectacular of railway walks, the Monsal Trail in Derbyshire. It runs from Bakewell to a point near Buxton, following the line of the Wye valley. At its opening in 1863, it was widely but not universally welcomed. John Ruskin had this to say:

> There was a rocky valley between Buxton and Bakewell, once upon a time, divine as the Vale of Tempe; you might have seen the Gods there morning and evening – Apollo and all the sweet Muses of the light – walking in fair procession on the lawns of it, and to and fro among the pinnacles of its crags. You cared neither for Gods nor grass, but for cash (which you did not know the way to get); you thought you would get it by what The Times calls 'Railroad Enterprise'. You Enterprised a Railroad through the valley – you blasted its rocks away, heaped thousands of tons of shale into its lovely stream. The valley is gone, and the Gods with it; and now, every fool in Buxton can be at Bakewell in half-an-hour; and every fool in Bakewell at Buxton; which you think a lucrative process of exchange – you Fools Everywhere.

Ruskin would no doubt be happy to know that the fools are back to walking again, and he might even be prepared to admit that time has mellowed the old line so that it now seems as natural a part of the dales scenery as the stone walls that climb across the hillsides. And although Ruskin was not unduly impressed by railway financiers, he might have had a grudging word of praise for

the railway engineers who contrived to cross the valley, but only through the construction of two viaducts and four tunnels. The tunnels have proved a nuisance to walkers, however, for they have been closed off leaving the actual railway walk as four separate lengths. But on one of those lengths, in Monsal Dale, one can still see and appreciate the way in which the engineers overcame the problems set by the lie of the land. Running north, the line disappears into a short tunnel just before Monsal Head, emerging to run over a magnificent stone viaduct, after which it clings to the side of the hill on a ledge cut into the slope before disappearing into yet another tunnel.

Monsal Dale viaduct is not one of the greatest and most impressive viaducts, though its setting is as lovely as any you will find – and it is certainly one of the finest to be met with on a railway walk. In some cases, such as the Castle Eden Walkway in Cleveland, the walk is interrupted by a gap caused by the demolition of a viaduct, in this case the once mighty Thorpe viaduct. Those with a taste for a little detective work, who feel they would like to find the traces of the old Leeds to Thirsk line can make their way to a spot to the south of Harrogate, where they will find the track bed of the old route – above which soars the mighty Crimple viaduct, which still carries the line from Harrogate to Leeds. Another interesting viaduct is met by those who walk the Dolgellau branch line to Morfa Mawddach, which ends by the Cambrian Railway's bridge which takes the main line across the estuary to Barmouth. It may lack the height and majesty of Crimple, but it is over 800 feet (243 metres) long and is unusual

Railway engineering at its most spectacular: Crimple viaduct still carries trains on their way between Leeds and Harrogate, but it crosses the track of the disused Leeds to Thirsk line.

for Britain in being built of timber. There is one further possibility for the future – even if it is a possibility few of us are keen to contemplate – that the Settle-Carlisle line will be closed and a path laid across the massive Ribblehead viaduct. It lies beneath the shadow of Pen-y-Ghent, but is certainly not dwarfed by its neighbour. In its majestic setting it represents one of the finest monuments to the engineers of a century ago.

Tunnels are less obviously impressive than viaducts, though their construction encompassed great engineering problems and, all too often, dangers and hardships for the work force on an equally large scale. There were two tunnels built at Woodhead in Cheshire in the nineteenth century and, in the making of the first of these, thirty-two workers were killed, 140 seriously wounded, and many more suffered badly from the unhealthy conditions in the dark, dank hole in the ground. There were fewer accidents in the making of the second tunnel, but the death toll was even higher, for cholera spread through the ramshackle shanty town that was the navvies' home. At the height of the epidemic, forty men died in a single night. In Otley churchyard, near Bramhope tunnel on the main line from Leeds, is a memorial to the unnumbered and anonymous men who died in that endeavour. It is a sobering thought that the routes we walk for pleasure were so hardly won. Not that, for obvious reasons, many railway walks include tunnels – spending time in the dripping dark is not everyone's idea of fun. There are, however, a number of short tunnels, of which one of the most interesting can be found on a very early line of George Stephenson's, the Whitby and Pickering Railway. This was a horse-drawn line which was later superseded by the steam line which is now the North Yorkshire Moors Railway. The old tunnel can be seen at Grosmont and it is a very attractive feature, with castellated portals.

All these major engineering works were undertaken to provide level tracks on which trains could be run. But there is little point in going to all that trouble without providing somewhere for the trains to stop, to load up with goods and passengers. The origins of the first railways as adjuncts to rivers and canals can be seen in the language of the first lines. In 1831, Joseph Priestley published a work generally known as 'Navigable Rivers and Canals', though its full title is *Historical Account of the Navigable Rivers, Canals and Railways throughout Great Britain*. Although it was published at the start of the steam railway age, railways were tacked on as something of an afterthought, but they are all here with details of Acts of Parliament, carriage rates, and so on. Look up the Stockton and Darlington Railway and you will find that '. . . lords of manors and owners of land on the line may erect wharfs and take the following wharfage rates. . .'. It was common for goods to be stored at wharves, just as they were on rivers, while passengers boarded their transport outside inns, just as other coaching passengers did. Nowhere will you find a mention of what we now regard as an essential part of the railway scene – the station. That only appeared with the completion of the Liverpool and Manchester Railway. The original Manchester terminus, now home to the Manchester Museum of Science and Industry, can lay claim to being the oldest surviving passenger station, though it only filled that role briefly before being converted for goods traffic. But, with its completion, the passenger station had arrived.

It is rare for an abandoned railway to boast anything especially grand in the way of stations: architectural splendours were reserved for important city sites where they served to remind the citizens – and investors – of the magnificent achievements of that particular company. Elsewhere, stations were modest, almost homely places – often it seems built in a quiet, domestic style to reassure anxious country folk that there was nothing to fear from railway travel. Popular songs of the time, however, expressed different sentiments:

But some poor simple souls may say
'Tis a dangerous thing to travel this way:
If the rail give way or the boiler burst,
There's nothing on earth can save us.
The money we paid from our poor pockets
May send us in the air like rockets.
Our heads as empty as water buckets,
Our precious eyes knocked out the sockets.

But the familiar, cottage-like station was there to comfort all passengers, to convince them that no such disasters were likely to occur. And just as country cottages change in style from region to region, so too do country stations. The railways of Britain were built by a myriad of different companies, each with ideas of its own. It is this splendid diversity which makes the prospect of finding an old station preserved – or, at least, not totally destroyed – such an attraction on a railway walk.

On some lines, the authorities who have taken them over and turned them into footpaths have made a special effort to keep and restore the old stations. Fine examples are Hadlow Road Station on the Wirral line and Tintern Station. Both represent the country cottage style of architecture, as snug and cosy as any rural retreat. They also represent exercises in nostalgia, a fossilized station stopped for ever at that moment in time when the line closed in the case of Hadlow Road. Tintern Station looks further back in time, but has much the same atmosphere. The booking hall stands ready to issue tickets for trains that will never come: advertising hoardings announce products for sale at prices that now seem to belong less to the recent past as to some dimly remembered period of history. The restorers have set out to capture an atmosphere and have, on the whole, succeeded even if certain vital ingredients will now be forever missing – the sight, the smell, and the sound of steam.

Elsewhere, old stations have been demolished, converted into private houses or to other uses. Some remain, it seems, as little more than a faint memory. At Blackmoor Gate, on the old Lynton and Barnstaple line, the main indication that this was ever a railway station is provided by the pub sign of the Old Station, though other memories are also stirring here. In the grounds, a small, square, stone building stands beneath the remains of a water pipe, marking the spot where locomotives once filled their boilers and, in the tiny building, is a railway museum which also serves to promote the activities of the group who are planning to reopen part of the line. Though their working days have ended, some stations still retain strong railway connections. One of the oldest is North Road, Darlington which provides a magnificent setting for a fine collection of locomotives and rolling stock. This is an obvious railway use, but there is considerable diversity of use – including use as a holiday home. Alton Station is unusual in having a somewhat exotic appearance, the architect having selected an Italianate style for his building. Where many country stations seem to be overgrown cottages, Alton contrives to look like a Florentine church. But, continuing the ecclesiastical theme, surely the oddest of all such conversions must be Walsingham Station on the abandoned Wells and Fakenham Railway. It now serves as a Russian Orthodox church, complete with miniature onion dome above the entrance. Services are held in the booking hall.

Stations are the most obvious relics of the vanished life of the railway, but by no means the only signs. Lines were usually supplied with small halts, which are now often seen as isolated platforms, or there may be no more than a pile of rubble to mark the spot where a few wind-blown passengers once waited for the local stopping train. Signals and signal boxes are occasional survivors and they certainly represent an important part of railway history. Strangely, they were rather late arrivals on the scene. Until the late 1850s, traffic was largely regulated by allowing suitable time gaps between trains using the same track: which was fine provided nothing went wrong with the train in front. The electric telegraph enabled the far more satisfactory block-working system to be introduced. Each line of a double track was divided into blocks, and no train would be allowed into a block until its predecessor had cleared the section. In 1856, John Saxby further improved safety by introducing a system linking points and signals, so that a signal could not be turned to 'clear' unless the points were correctly set. This system, based on the familiar semaphore signal remained in use for a very long time, and can still be seen on many preserved lines. I can even recall working as a porter on a main line station when, on the early shift, my first task was to walk down the line and fill the oil lamps in the signals outside the station.

Sidings often appear as reminders of the other part of the commercial life of the railways, the carriage of freight. Warehouses can be found where goods were held ready for loading, and lines snaked off into the heart of many an industrial concern. I have frequently found remains of old railways while looking at other industrial remnants. While studying the remains of the old copper and tin industries of Cornwall, I came across extensive evidence of mineral railways, even on the wild slopes of Bodmin Moor. I recall also pausing to look at the ruined engine house of the East Calstock copper mine on the Cornish side of the Tamar. Across the road was what appeared to be, and indeed was, a water tower while alongside it was a well-preserved engine shed. I had come upon the remains of the East Cornwall Mineral Railway. This was the point where the rope-worked incline down to the river met the

Opposite Blackmoor Gate, once a station on the Lynton and Barnstaple Light Railway is now a pub. This little building, with the remains of the water tower, is a railway museum and marks the first stirrings of a restoration movement on this beautiful line.

TICKET
OFFICE

LYNTON & BARNSTAPLE
RAILWAY ASSN.
MUSEUM
OPEN TODAY

conventional narrow-gauge railway. And narrow-gauge lines, industrial and even passenger routes, such as the Lynton and Barnstaple, are another source of routes for walkers.

The forerunner of all such lines was the Festiniog Railway – now distinguished by an extra Welsh 'f' as the Ffestiniog – which was built as a horse railway and opened in 1836. In terms of engineering it was something of a triumph with its rock cuttings and sharp bends carrying the line from the slate mines and quarries of Blaenau Ffestiniog to the harbour at Porthmadog. The final stage of the journey involved the construction of a causeway across the bay. Because of the difficult mountain terrain, the gauge was restricted to a diminutive 1 foot 11½ inches (59.5 centimetres). There were obvious difficulties in working locomotives over such a narrow track, and the first trials were graphically described by the railway's manager, C. E. Spooner, in his classic book *Narrow Gauge Railways*. A certain amount of civil engineering was required before trials could begin with steam locomotives in the 1860s. The first experiments with a conventional engine, the *Little Giant*, sound quite alarming. As the pistons worked alternately on either side of the engine, they set up an oscillation, so that the locomotive began to sway from side to side. This bobbing and weaving motion, earned the dimunitive engine its nickname, 'The Boxer'. The maximum speed was around 8 miles per hour which, Spooner noted, was '. . . the greatest at which it is possible to run without incurring the risk of breaking the springs, or loosening the driver's teeth'. Then followed a run with the strange-looking double Fairlie locomotives, which look very much as if two identical engines have been run into each other back to back and then welded together. These engines are still in use on the Ffestiniog and are more accurately described as double-bogied engines with the cab in the middle. With these there was none of the old oscillation of the *Little Giant*. The narrow-gauge railway was now declared a complete success. The Fairlie design was never widely used, but the steam locomotive and the narrow gauge railway had, with their help, been successfully united.

It is still possible to see the whole of Ffestiniog history on the site. The most obvious features are the locomotives, including the Fairlies. At Porthmadog there is a reminder of the earlier days of railway life in the form of a dandy cart in which the horse rode along those sections where its efforts were not needed to pull the train. But, although this is principally a route for steam enthusiasts, there is something here for the walker as well. In bringing the line back to Blaenau Ffestiniog, the modern engineers constructed a spiralling route above Lyn Ystradau, and a new tunnel on a new alignment brings the route back to the original at Tanygrisiau. But that original route between Dduallt and Tanygrisiau has been opened up as a footpath, so that one can walk along a route on which old stone sleeper blocks may still be seen while, higher up the hill, a hundred or more years old locomotive can be seen working hard on the most recently constructed passenger line in Britain. There can surely be few places where so many layers of rail history are packed together in the one spot.

That early success on the Ffestiniog led to some spectacular narrow-gauge lines being built overseas, and there was a renewed interest in the idea with the passing of the Light Railways Act of 1896, which allowed such lines to be constructed without the huge inconvenience and expense of obtaining an individual Act of Parliament. The idea was to help fill in the gaps in the railway networks – gaps which mattered to local communities, but were not always so interesting to investors. Some of these were built to a narrow gauge, such as the Lynton and Barnstaple already mentioned which, although it has left us some fine structures, notably the curving, 70-foot (21-metre) high Chelfham viaduct, was not a great success. In fact, the line was closed in 1935 after less than fifty years of use. Some of its contemporaries were, if anything, even less successful – the Leek and Manifold, which never seemed to have the slightest chance of finding passengers, being a classic example. But the promoters' loss has proved the walkers' gain as it is now one of the most popular of railway walks (*see* page 100).

The light railways represented the final stage of expansion of the rail network in Britain: from then on, contraction was to be the rule, apart from some rather specialized areas, such as underground and industrial lines. The latter were of considerable importance to many concerns, though not all builders of industrial railways worked on the scale of the famous Bass brewery of Burton-on-Trent, which had 16 miles of privately owned track, with their own locomotives and rolling stock. Memories of those days of beery trains are preserved in the Bass Museum, where a brewery train still stands on the tracks – but it is only a memory. The turning point came at the end of World War I. The men who had survived the trenches came home and began to look for work: at much the same time a large number of cheap army surplus trucks and lorries appeared on the market. There were few regulations governing road transport and many an ex-serviceman saw a bright and profitable future in road haulage. The Road Traffic Act of 1930, regulating the use of commercial road vehicles, brought some relief to the railways, and a second Act of 1933 helped still more, but really it was too late. Competition ate away at the profits of many companies, especially the smaller ones. The argument over what might have been and what should have been still goes on, and I have no intention of rehearsing it here. The facts are that the railways were in decline and, Beeching or no Beeching, some were bound to go.

So it was that many lines were closed, abandoned, and left to rot. The process will almost certainly continue and, even while this book was being completed, the last train ran from Oxford to Abingdon and the line was closed. To the true railway enthusiast the prospect that a much-loved line might be converted to footpath or cycle track offers, at best, scant comfort. Railways were designed to carry trains and it is often said that without that traffic they can be no more than pale reflections of the vanished reality. This is true in some respects, for any railway, whether from the tramway age or the steam age, is a compound of the two, distinct elements. The first is the route itself with all its bridges, viaducts, cuttings and banks, its signals and stations. The second element is

Closure: this diesel unit carried the last train load of passengers that would ever travel the branch line from Radley to Abingdon. The line was finally closed to traffic in 1984. What will happen to it now?

the moving part of locomotives and rolling stock which brought the line to life. It is undeniable that where the latter have gone, a vital ingredient has been lost. Yet, fortunately, we human beings are blessed with imaginations, so that, as we walk down some lonely, remote cutting, we can still hear in our minds the shrill blast of the whistle or, as the line tilts up a gentle slope, we can envisage the asthmatic wheezing of a little tank engine hauling a load of clanking trucks behind it. For many of us this is a major part of the appeal of a walk down the line and for those who share that outlook, there will always be a case for delving back into the working history of the abandoned route.

It is not strictly necessary to take even the slightest interest in railway history to enjoy the walks, but this brief resumé of some of the highlights of the past made visible through the physical remains will, I hope, convince many walkers that a knowledge of the railway past will enhance the pleasure to be obtained from walking the disused lines today. There will be many who will continue to regard the lines as happy accidents, providing corridors through towns or easily traceable tracks through the country. But for me the appeal will always lie, in part, with those memories of the past. As I walk the disused railway I seem often to feel that at my elbow there is another walker, the ghost of a sturdy gentleman, perhaps somewhat incongruously clad in top hat and frock coat, but shod in good stout boots designed for rough walking. Sticking from the tail of his coat are maps and charts and, as he walks, he casts a keen eye around him, taking in every dip and hollow, aware of each change in the surface of the land. He is the engineer, the man who decreed that the line should follow precisely this route, that a bridge should be built here, a station there. The railways were never impersonal creations: they reflect the tastes and opinion of individuals. And, just as each engineer has a particular personality, so too each line has its own individual and distinct character. And in that lies their greatest charm.

BACK TO NATURE

4

It is a commonplace to talk of things going back to nature, yet this is precisely what has happened in the case of the oldest railway lines. The tramways rarely contained much in the way of engineering works, as they tended to follow the natural contours of the land. Even the inclines, though they were worked by the huge beam engines of the day, have done little to disturb the landscape as a whole. In the great majority of cases, a few tumbled stones are all that remain of the mighty engine houses, and the stone sleeper blocks are the only indications that a railway ever existed. In some cases, there were, as we have seen, tunnels, bridges, banks, and cuttings, but nothing on the scale of the later age. The tramways were surface markers, easily removed and easily forgotten, soon overgrown by the local vegetation. Back to nature they have gone indeed. The same cannot be said of the railways of the steam locomotive period. The disused lines may rapidly become overgrown, but not necessarily in a 'natural' way, for the old routes were, from the start, very 'unnatural' intrusions into the landscape. The ending of traffic has not meant that they have simply been absorbed back into the surrounding environment. They retain individual characteristics which declare them as man made, essentially different from the country through which they pass. If we go back to the first line, described in Chapter 1, the Didcot, Newbury and Southampton Railway, it should become a little clearer as to what this means.

The track ran out of Didcot on an embankment built up from material excavated out of the cutting through the Downs, and that is a fact of great significance in terms of plant life. The countryside on either side of the bank is a flat plain of sands and gravels, providing an acid soil on which the typical plants of such an environment are found. But the embankment itself is quite different, an alkali strip stretching out a thin finger through the acid soils, for this is the soil of the downland. This is not the only change the bank has brought to plant life. Standing as it does high above the surrounding land on a north-east to south-west alignment, it presents one side to the sun and consigns the other to the shadows. Any weekend gardener will know the effects of such a contrast, with the sunny side flourishing and the other retarded.

The cutting provides an even more dramatic change of environment than the embankment. Slicing deep into the chalk, it provides a geological specimen, cut open for inspection. But over the years, its character has changed. While the line was in use, with regular maintenance of the ballast, and drains well cleared, it provided a dry path through the hills – but not any longer. It still acts as a drain, but now as a far less efficient one. The bottom of the cutting has become in many places a miniature wetland, a form of environment that is becoming increasingly rare in Britain. Elsewhere marsh and fen are being drained to meet the supposed needs of agriculture. Here the process is reversed. What was once drained and dry now supports colonies of typical wetland plants and, even on the comparatively dry cutting sides, the vegetation is very different from that of the surrounding land. Saplings have taken vigorous life, and bracken and rhododendrons have found a home.

Beyond the cutting, where one might expect to find least change on the line, there is still a very obvious difference between what one might call railway plants and the other species of the area. Though the tracks have gone, the stone ballast remains, but is all but vanished from sight beneath a rich growth of mosses and lichens. But what is a railway plant and what is a native plant of the region? The distinction is not always obvious. One plant which is now thought of as a common British resident is really little better than a foreign hobo that has hitched a ride on many a train. This is the Oxford ragwort, a bushy herb with yellow flowers. It was brought from Italy, where it grew naturally on the volcanic ash of Etna and Vesuvius and was given a home in the Botanic Garden beside the Cherwell in Oxford. There it might well have stayed, nodding at the drifting punts of a summer afternoon, for Oxford offered very little in the way of volcanic environments – until the railway came. Cinder, clinker, and ash spread out along the line of the Great Western Railway and the seeds of the ragwort suddenly found that they had a home from home. Down the line the ragwort spread and prospered, courtesy of the G.W.R.

Other plants may not have made quite such dramatic bids for freedom as the Oxford ragwort in its escape from the confines of the Botanic Gardens, but they too have escaped domesticity for a life in the wild. One of the features of many a small country station was the well-kept station garden. With the line closed and the station demolished and fallen into ruin, the roses have rioted and the well-manicured trees and shrubs become unkempt and coarse. It is a useful reminder of just how quickly the cultured, domestic plant can return to its wild beginnings. What is true of the one line, is true to a greater or lesser degree of all disused railways. They have become types of linear nature reserves with special characteristics all their own and with a rich variety of plant life. In taking over old lines and making them available to walkers, some local authorities have acknowledged this fact.

An excellent example of a disused line that has been turned specifically into a nature reserve can be seen in West Sussex, between Slinfold and Rudgwick. It is particularly well used by schools, and the visitors are given detailed notes and questionnaires on the route. Much of this line lies in a cutting where the Weald clay was covered by chalk to prevent land slip, providing a well-drained, sheltered region where a variety of plants now flourish. Many of these are very much what one would expect to find on such a route – brambles, nettles, and willowherb, scarcely exotic species. The trees are also commonplace – oak, hornbeam, hazel, and sallow. But there are also a number of special railway residents to study and enjoy. St John's-wort is not an uncommon plant, but it provides a brilliant yellow flecking to the south-facing bank in summer. The purple flowers of the hairy violet and the sweet fruit of the wild strawberry add their touch of colour and proclaim the chalky nature of the soil. The north-facing slope has the most interesting plants, in the shape of spotted orchids. Among the trees, there is also one which almost certainly has a purely railway origin, for the solitary apple no doubt owes its being to an apple core casually dispatched from a passing train.

This particular strip has been developed especially as a nature walk with an educational purpose but, even in those areas which are intended for use by the general public, a real effort has often been made to give an indication at least of the special nature of the plant life. On the Pencaitland Railway walk, for example (*see* page 105), a series of colour-coded posts are being installed to show the different forms of plant life to look out for along the way. On recently abandoned lines, you can see the process of plant establishment, and the Pencaitland markers are intended to differentiate between dwarf species and those which are just beginning a period of steady growth. This is especially useful when looking at trees, and what a blessing the old lines prove to be. Trees and hedgerows seem under constant threat in Britain – the former because of the steady advancement of the regiments of conifers, the latter by destruction by farmers who prefer big fields and the simplicity of wire. Along the line of the Pencaitland, birch stands by Scots pine, oak by willow – there is a diversity which is seldom found elsewhere.

This brings us to what seems to be one of the main virtues of the railway lines – and brings us also to a rather splendid paradox. Our countryside is undergoing a period of rapid change, the likes of which have not been seen since the enclosure movement of the eighteenth and nineteenth centuries. Fields are expanding, hedge-rows vanishing, mixed woodland gives way to conifer plantations, wetlands are drained, moorland is ploughed. In short, the diversity of the country, which is its chief glory, is being diminished, often to satisfy the narrowest of commercial interests – conformity rules. Yet it is these railways which once helped to spread conformity over the land which now form the secret passages along which the old, splendidly muddled rag-bag of species are being re-established. The old hedgerow plants, which were grubbed out and replaced by post and wire fences, are growing again along the cuttings. A huge variety of wild flowers can be found, representative of many different habitats. Not all of this is the result of nature taking over, for humans have sometimes had to take a hand to ensure a balance, to keep the mix rich and varied. Some might argue that nature will always sort things out perfectly well without intervention but the authorities responsible for the railway walks in the Peak District National Park have not found matters to be quite that simple. They found that on the Tissington and High Peak trails, sycamore, which was not a native to the region, had developed along the tracks and was thriving at the expense of other species. Nature can be avaricious, and the corollary to the law of the survival of the fittest is the disappearance of the less fit. Control was essential if a good mixture was to be maintained. Often, those plants which might be thought of as more than capable of looking after themselves, proved to need a helping hand. If, for example, you want to have an attractive grass verge to the line, some sort of control again proves necessary – but what sort of control? How do you keep that control without obtrusion? Sheep seemed a good notion, but the coarse grass proved too much for them. Bullocks did a much better job, but terrified some of the walkers. The answer proved less than wholly satisfactory: burning back the rough grasses in rotation. If no-one is very happy with this answer, all agree that the aims of the authorities are basically sound: to maintain as diverse a plant life as possible, representative of both the district through which the walk passes and the special, artificially created characteristics of the line itself.

Anyone walking an old railway will soon become aware of this rich diversity of plant life, and there is no need to be a specialist in, or even to know anything about the subject at all, to appreciate it. The plants provide colour and fragrance; they produce patterns on the land which shift and change with the changes of the light. They can break the monotony of too much of the modern country landscape, and bring a touch of the wild to the heart of the town. But it is not just for this that the plants are welcome. We might only want to look at them – other creatures have to live on them. Remote now from the busy world, the lines provide peaceful habitats for insects, birds, and other animals.

The natural history of the railways is not strictly divisible into compartments, and most of us who walk the line for pleasure do not attempt to make such divisions. We note an attractive flower, spot a colourful butterfly, or pause to listen to the song of the lark. And we are quite right not to make strict divisions, for the natural world exists as a complex, closely woven fabric: the flower attracts the insect, the insect attracts the bird. The animal life and the plant life are interdependent. The wide variety of plants to be seen on the Slinfold line, for example, is matched by an equally wide selection of insects. Not all are equally endearing – few walkers would be attracted to the cutting by the information that it is well endowed with hoverflies despite their harmless nature and interest to the entomologist! In spring and early summer, however, all the following butterflies have been recorded: brimstone, peacock, comma, large white, green-veined white, white admiral, gate-keeper, meadow brown, and small skipper. It is very noticeable on many walks that the concentration of these attractive little creatures is much greater than in their surrounding countryside where pesticides have wreaked their damage. A similar story can be repeated when one turns to the bird life of the lines.

The great attractions for birds are the proliferation of plant cover and the comparative lack of disturbance. It really does seem quite odd that these railways which, when first constructed, forced themselves through the country as noisy, dirty routes, now provide havens of peace. Yet so it is. The Pencaitland line has records of birds as well as butterflies, and to date fifty-eight different species have been spotted. Few authorities have kept such scrupulous records of birds seen, and heard, on their lines, but many have noted their more attractive visitors which their human visitors might care to watch out for. There are resident colonies, ranging from blackbirds to yellowhammers and a mixed bunch of callers

Opposite The sheltered sides of a cutting on the Whitby to Scarborough line make a splendid habitat for a rich collection of flowers and flowering grasses.

from blackcaps to waxwings. And this is not just something that matters to the ornithologist, for could anything do more to lift the spirits of a walker than suddenly to find a lark rising from the undergrowth to hover in song high above, in a blue sky – and those who answer, 'Yes, the sight of an open pub,' will be drummed out of the Keats Appreciation Society.

The railway has also provided a prime residential development area for wild animals. Embankments must have seemed like luxury flats in the making for the local rabbit population which soon set up home there and in the sides of cuttings. Wander down any railway today and you will find ample evidence of their presence – and probably see more than one of them scurrying away, white tail bobbing. Smaller animals – mice, rats, voles – find the railways equally enticing, and they in their turn provide an attraction for larger carnivores. As the small animals gathered, so the predators moved in. Stoats are not uncommon, while the fox is now a regular railway traveller, not merely out in the country but on disused lines in the towns as well. Quite an urban character, the fox, these days, for he has found the left-overs of human life to be just as tasty and nutritious as living prey, and far less trouble to acquire. Residents along the line through Muswell Hill (*see* page 148) have become accustomed to midnight raids on their dustbins. The fox has become quite bold in his scavenging raids and, it seems, less concerned by the proximity to man. I recall walking down that old line preceded by a strutting fox, his brush held high, that occasionally turned his head to see what I was up to, but otherwise seemed quite unperturbed by my presence.

Those who keep eyes and ears open as they walk – and do not make too much noise themselves – stand a fair chance of seeing some wildlife in the course of their travels. Some lines, however, offer a chance of something a little more unusual than rabbits and squirrels. The Castle Eden walkway in Cleveland, for example, offers the chance of watching roe deer. And, at the very least, the self-contained world of the railway offers an opportunity to watch the farmer and his livestock without incurring the wrath of either. A high embankment is certainly one of the better viewpoints for observing the behaviour of a large, well-horned bull. And there is always the chance that patient observation will reveal traces of some of the rarer species. Recently I discovered a railway that had been adopted by a family of badgers, which could be seen leaving their sett in the failing light of early evening.

It is not necessary to be able to recognize soil types, name plants, and identify the different bird songs to enjoy a walk down the line, any more than it is for any other walk in town or country. Nevertheless, the old railways do now provide an unusually rich habitat, all the more welcome in these days when urban growth and mechanized, intensive farming are steadily removing such habitats elsewhere. Few of us are specialists in any sense of the word, but most of us are at least aware of the pleasures that derive from diversity in the countryside. The railways do provide just that diversity in good measure, and it is greatly encouraging to read through piles of leaflets describing railway walks, as I have done in preparing this book, and find how much emphasis local authorities have placed on the notion of the lines as linear nature parks. But, of course, the greatest threat to the concept of the old railway as conservation areas comes from ourselves, those who use the facilities. It is we, alas, who pick the flowers, discard our wrappers and leave cans and broken bottles as potential maimers of the wildlife. Mr Archie Mathieson, Senior Ranger on the Pencaitland Railway Walk puts his advice to users as succinctly as anyone: 'Leave nothing but goodwill, kill nothing but time, take nothing but photographs.' It would be pleasant to think that all railway walkers followed his advice.

Once the little marker post passed on vital information to engine drivers, but now it is steadily being absorbed into the luxuriant under-growth of the old Wye Valley line.

5 GETTING UNDER WAY

From the start, a distinction must be made between the tramway walks and the railway walks. In the latter case, the route is usually well defined, but the problem facing the would-be tramway walker is more easily stated than resolved – first find your tramway. The present 1:50 000 series of Ordnance Survey maps usually shows the routes of old railways in some detail, but rarely those of the earlier age. One can just sit down and do one's own research – scour old maps for lines which are marked where no lines exist today, but this is not a very satisfactory approach. A good deal of time can be spent hunting in areas where no tramway ever existed. There is, it is true, a deal of satisfaction to be obtained from making your very own discovery, but the chances are that someone else has already made the discovery before you. On the whole, it is better to start by taking advantage of the works of others. The classic book on the subject is Baxter's *Stone Blocks and Iron Rails* but many of the regional industrial archaeological guides also give details of old tramway routes. There are also a number of guides published by local societies which contain a wealth of detail. Unfortunately, as walking old tramways is not what one might call a popular activity, local tourist authorities seldom have much information to offer. A notable exception is the Welsh Tourist Board which has laid out a number of industrial trails, many of which contain details of old tramway routes.

There is, then, a deal of information available to those prepared diligently to search it out. Some, however, might prefer to go right back to basics and do their own research, and for them an obvious starting point is the first edition of the Ordnance Survey map, a modern edition of which is available for England and Wales but not, alas, for Scotland. Routes linked to canals can often be traced from canal maps, or located on the ground. Those travelling the Macclesfield Canal north from Kidsgrove will soon come across a flat-topped bridge near Kent Green, which is in marked contrast to the more familiar hump-backed bridges of the inland waterways. A glance at the map will identify it as Bridge Number 91, Tramroad Bridge – an obvious starting point for exploration. Many canals are rich in tramway connections – the Caldon, the Macclesfield, and the Peak Forest are notable examples in England, while virtually all the Welsh canals have tramways associated with them. Details of many of these, together with other early railways, can be found in Joseph Priestley's *Navigable Rivers and Canals* of 1831, which is available in a modern edition. A word of warning here: the book mainly lists Acts of Parliament, and not all routes that were authorized were actually built.

There is not enough space in a short introduction to indicate all the means that can be used to trace these old lines. A glance at a detailed study, such as Gordon Rattenbury's *Tramroads of the Brecknock and Abergavenny Canal*, will give an idea of the vast

amount of documents that are available for study. Happily, for those who prefer walking to recording, enough routes have been described to provide many, many excursions. Even so, having a description of a route is by no means the same thing as being able to locate it on the ground. Some routes are easy enough to follow, but some very much less so – and for many of us who enjoy the hunt, this is an essential part of the pleasure of tramway walking.

The first essential, once you have route details, is to equip yourself with map and compass – the 1:50 000 Ordnance Survey map should prove adequate for most purposes. Both items are necessary, for you might well find yourself in open country at a spot where the line you thought you were following has apparently vanished without trace. I found myself on Bodmin Moor in just such a situation, but I was able to determine precisely where I was and where I should be heading. I was confident that the line would reappear, and so it did. After less than a mile's walking, the unmistakable stone blocks of a tramroad came into view. On such occasions a pair of binoculars can be very useful for, if you are straying off the straight and narrow, then a quick scan of the way ahead can put you right again.

Following the later railways of the steam age is, or should be, an altogether simpler matter, because they are generally well and clearly marked on the 1:50 000 maps. The task has been greatly eased recently by the publication of the *Complete British Railways Maps and Gazetteer from 1830–1981* by C J Wignall. This excellent book contains eighty-seven maps covering the whole of Britain and showing both existing and disused lines, the latter being colour coded to differentiate between early closures and those of the Beeching age. However, the presence of a disused line on a map is not an indication that the line is open to walkers. In the next chapter, you will find details of twenty-one railway walks in different parts of Britain where access is reasonably well assured and, in the gazetteer, there are brief notes on many more routes,

The line of the Haytor Granite Tramway is plain enough as it snakes across Dartmoor on a fine, clear day. But those who follow it out on to the moor should be aware of the dramatic changes that can occur in the region.

the great majority of which are tracks made available to walkers and, sometimes, cyclists and horse riders. Yet these still only represent a small fraction of the total length of disused railways in Britain. The fact that a line is not included in the gazetteer does not mean that walking is impossible or forbidden, merely that no official right of access exists. It is by no means a simple matter to find out who owns a stretch of land – nor is it necessary to go to great lengths to do so. Common sense is a great help. Ask nicely and politely if you can walk a line and, in most cases, you will be allowed to do so. Farmers who are often – and, it must be said, with good cause – jealous guardians of their land, tend to welcome railway walkers, because they keep well clear of crops. Walkers should, however, remember that old railway lines are not, in the vast majority of cases, routes along which they have any rights of way at all. If the landowner really wishes to turf them off, then off they must be turfed. There are helpful owners who put up 'Welcome' signs, and those who scatter barbed wire entanglements and 'Keep Off' signs in all directions. It is sad that this should be so for, in many cases, there is no sound reason why a way should not be opened up, but such is the way of the world. And, unfortunately, there is no indication on the map that obstacles will not be found to block the path, either in the form of the 'Private – Keep Out' notices, or collapsed bridges or filled-in cuttings.

It should be clear then that setting out to walk old railway lines is not necessarily the simple matter that it might seem at first glance. Not all routes are easily accessible: some indeed are not accessible at all. It is as well to be aware of the problems but, at the same time, one does not want to give the impression that such walks are so difficult to achieve that the only sensible decision is to give up the whole notion. Difficulties are there to be surpassed and, once they are overcome, then the reward seems all the greater. But these problems of access and ownership represent only a part of the barrier which confronts not just the railway walker, but all who set out on long-distance treks.

No-one enjoys an uncomfortable walk. Blisters and cuts do nothing to increase our pleasure; hunger and thirst make us irritable and bad tempered. It is very tempting to underestimate what is required of the explorer of old railway routes. After all, it is in the nature of railways to run along more or less level routes which, after closure, remain as easy, level walkways. But the ground underfoot may be far from ideal. In a cutting, for example, if the ballast is retained, the way will be stony and uneven; if the ballast is removed, it can rapidly decline into a quagmire. It is a 'heads you win – tails I lose' situation. The most common mistake made by railway walkers is to set out with feet inadequately shod. It might seem unnecessary to go to the expense of buying good, solid walking boots, but not to do so is a false economy. Anyone who has ever had the very satisfying experience of trudging well shod through mud and puddle while their companions have hopped, shuffled, and executed strange balletic movements in the vain hope of keeping their feet dry, will appreciate the advantage of a good pair of boots. The investment is repaid time after time. Whenever you want to scramble down an embankment or climb the sides of a cutting you will bless the fact that you are well shod; whenever you squelch through mud or clamber over shifting shale, you will feel the same. The same is true of other expenses incurred on equipment. Anyone planning a long railway walk would be well advised to set off in the expectation that the weather will be foul. This is especially true of those who walk the upland lines, where weather changes can be both sudden and dramatic. Railway walks may lead you quietly into the hills, but they provide no guarantees that the hills will be gentle with the walker. You may never need extra food to tide you over; you may never need to blow a whistle to indicate the spot where you are crouched, cold, miserable and lost, sheltering behind a boulder – but you will never regret carrying that extra food, that whistle, or any other safety device that will help you to survive an unlooked-for accident in the wilder parts of the country. Never worry about being thought over-fussy and silly – among those who did worry about their image are a few who will never worry about anything else again.

It is true that the railway walker is seldom, if ever, subject to any great privations, but life can become unnecessarily uncomfortable. It is in the nature of railway walks to be linear. You can plan an ordinary country stroll and arrange to end up where you started – but railways progress from A to B and do not return to A again, but rather progress to C, D, and E. As a lot of us arrive at the starting point by car, we need to be able to return to the vehicle at the end of the day. Even those true enthusiasts who go everywhere by train must remember that their walk only exists because the trains no longer run. So back to the start we all must go, which usually involves more footwork or a bus. So, while planning a walk, keep public transport in mind – and bus timetables are not difficult to acquire. (There is a list of tourist boards where travel information can be obtained in the Appendix.)

It is all too easy in an introduction such as this to give the impression that the whole project of railway walking is fraught with difficulties. This is, quite simply, not the case and there are, in fact, few easier ways to penetrate to the peace of the country than by following a derelict line. And practical help is available from organizations such as the Railway Ramblers and the Branch Line Society. And even those who find the prospect of long walks a little too daunting can take comfort in the large number of short walks opened up by many authorities. Most of these walks – and especially those of the locomotive age – have a built-in advantage in that they keep to the very level routes. This makes them ideal not just for those who feel that they cannot cope with anything too strenuous, but also with those who are unable to cope with anything else – the disabled. A problem facing many disabled people is that of enjoying, as the able enjoy, the delights of the open air and the country. It is no simple matter to bump over rocky tracks in a wheel chair or to plough through mud on crutches – the railways provide a great potential for help. The conditions dictated by the needs of the steam locomotive are just those conditions which could prove of greatest value to the disabled. This has been recognized by some authorities. An outstanding example is to be found in the Snowdonia National Park, where the

The path of the Portland Railway makes an exciting walk, but one cannot help regretting that the trains no longer run out from Weymouth along the tracks beneath the cliffs.

old line along the Mawddach Estuary has been opened up with a very special provision for the disabled. All kinds of wheel chairs can use the route and a group has been kept in mind which rarely gets special consideration – the blind. To some it may seem that the blind can have little appreciation of the country but, if they cannot see, they can feel and hear. So, the route has been made accessible to them by the provision of hand rails, into which plaques have been inlaid with information about hazards ahead in a bilingual braille. Such facilities could, given good will and, of course, the finance, be repeated on many of our railway walks. It would be a great boon to thousands.

Walkers are not the only group to use old railways – increasingly they are being seen as suitable routes for cyclists. This book was written in the first place with walkers in mind but, in the course of covering the lines, I have become increasingly aware of how well and easily they can be adapted as cycle routes. Many have been opened up with cyclists in mind and, in the gazetteer, I have tried to indicate those lines which can be cycled as well as walked. I have, however, assumed a certain robustness on the part of both cycle and cyclist, for many of the tracks are, to put it mildly, a little on the rough side. A number of routes are also available as bridlepaths but, whatever form of transport is used – one's own feet and legs or those of another animal, the essential pleasures of railway 'walking' remain the same. Birds and flowers, trees and animals enhance the pleasures of a walk but, for most of us, it is that half-heard throb of a little tank engine labouring up a gentle slope that makes a railway walk unique.

TAKE TWENTY-ONE LINES

As a glance at the gazetteer at the back of the book will show, this represents only a tiny fraction of the mileage of old railways designated as walks, and an even smaller fraction of the total mileage of disused routes. The twenty-one have been selected because, between them, they seem to give a reasonable notion of the range and variety of such walks. They encompass tramways and railways, urban and rural routes, short walks and long. They are almost all 'official' walks, duly approved by local authorities – those which are not are clearly indicated as such, and have been included because of their uniquely interesting features – and unique is certainly the word to apply to the first of these journeys down old lines.

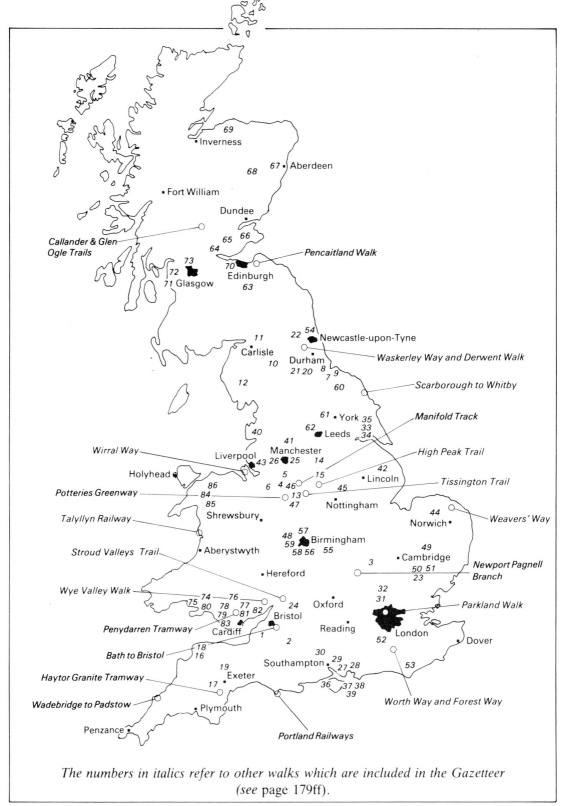

69
Inverness

68 *67* Aberdeen

Fort William

Dundee

65 66
64
Callander & Glen
Ogle Trails Pencaitland Walk

73
72
71 Glasgow *70*
Edinburgh
63

11 *22 54* Newcastle-upon-Tyne
Carlisle *10* Durham Waskerley Way and Derwent Walk
21 20 *8* *7 9*
12 *60* Scarborough to Whitby

61 York *35* Manifold Track
62 *33*
40 Leeds *34*
41 High Peak Trail
Wirral Way *26 25* *14*
Liverpool *43* Manchester *42*
Holyhead *5* *15* Lincoln Tissington Trail
86 *6* *4 46* *45*
Potteries Greenway *84* *13*
85 *47* Nottingham *44* Weavers' Way
Talyllyn Railway Shrewsbury Norwich
48 57 *49*
Stroud Valleys Trail *59* Birmingham Cambridge Newport Pagnell
Aberystwyth *58 56* *55* *50 51* Branch
3 *23*
Hereford
Wye Valley Walk *32*
74 76 *31* Parkland Walk
75 *77* *24* Oxford
80 *78* *82*
Penydarren Tramway *79 81* Bristol Reading *52* London Dover
Cardiff *1* *2* *53*
Bath to Bristol *18*
16 *19*
Haytor Granite Tramway *30*
Southampton *29* Worth Way and Forest Way
17 Exeter *27 28*
Wadebridge to Padstow *36* *37 38*
Plymouth *39*

Penzance Portland Railways

*The numbers in italics refer to other walks which are included in the Gazetteer
(see page 179ff).*

THE WALKS

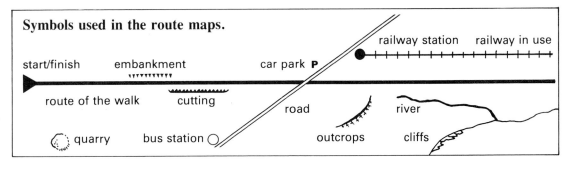

Symbols used in the route maps.

railway station   railway in use

start/finish   embankment   car park **P**

route of the walk   cutting

road   river

quarry   bus station   outcrops   cliffs

HAYTOR GRANITE TRAMWAY

Route   Circular route on Haytor Down, 4 miles
Maps   OS 191, Dartmoor one-inch Tourist Map
Access   Haytor road car park on minor road to south of Haytor

This is an extraordinary route, both for the wild beauty of its setting and for the nature of the old line itself for, although it was built in 1820, it looks back to the old rutted ways of the ancient world while still remaining recognizably a railway. It was built under the direction of George Templer to bring stone from the quarries high on Dartmoor to the Stover Canal at Teigngrace. Now there was never any doubt that some form of railway was the obvious answer to the problem, but Templer faced a difficulty: iron was not made in the region and the cost of bringing iron from other areas appeared prohibitive. But one thing they did have in plenty – stone, good hard granite. So why not forget about iron rails and build a system using granite rails? And that is precisely what was done, and the railway remains today as a monument to the durability of granite.

The easiest way for motorists to set about following the route is to walk down the road from the car park and then turn north up the road to Moretonhampstead. About a hundred metres up this road, a standing granite slab marks the beginning of the route. One set of rails can be seen leading off to the east, while the main track heads off across the moor towards the bold outline of the Haytor rocks. It is quite astonishing how well preserved the line remains, in spite of the traffic of the years rumbling laboriously over the stony way. The 'rails' set to a 4-foot 3-inch (1.29-metre) gauge consist of blocks up to 8 feet (2.43 metres) long, 9 inches (22.86 centimetres) wide, and 12½ inches (31.75 centimetres)

Opposite The extraordinary stone 'rails' of the Haytor Granite Tramway, running through the shallow cutting that is one of the few engineering features on the line.

deep, cut to an L shape in cross-section, like a conventional tramway. Along this route, hewn blocks from the quarry were dragged in trains of twelve waggons, each train pulled by a team of eighteen horses, harnessed one behind the other. The pulling was for the uphill journey: coming down hill, they were fastened behind the train to act as living brakes. It is hard now to envisage the scene, for the moor seems such a remote and almost desolate spot, far removed from the bustle of industry. It is a world of heather and coarse grass, wide prospects punctuated by the steep risings of rock and tor. The sound of blasting and hammering has long since been stilled, to be replaced by the summer song of the lark.

There is certainly no difficulty in following the line, for the stone rails form an almost continuous path across the moor, leading away towards the north of the tor itself, where the shattered rocks of a quarry soon become a distinctive feature of the skyline. In fact, the main line itself also passes north of the quarry, but a spur leads off towards it, branching at what one can only describe as a set of points. To those accustomed to conventional railways, it seems distinctly odd to find the whole thing reproduced in stone though here, of course, the 'points' were never switched. Trucks, it appears, were bodily heaved or levered from one set of rails to the next. The quarry branch line runs on a low embankment to the promontories of spoil below the rocks, but the main line continues in a shallow cutting round the foot of the hill towards Holwell Tor. This, in both the railway and the scenic sense, is the best of the line. Tremendous views open up towards Houndtor where the skyline is marked by a jagged fringe of grey rock, while up ahead the gentler slope of the moor still retains its sense of wildness. A solitary tree bent by the wind leans towards the stony summit of the tor, where a few hopeful cows grub out the coarse grass. Here, too, the stones of the track are especially well preserved, showing the imprint of the many wheels that, over the years, dug grooves down even into this hard rock. There are also a number of short spurs, providing passing places for two-way traffic on the single track. Mister Templer's tramway is a mightily durable and ingenious piece of work.

At Holwell Tor the line peters out and the walker is faced by the wide horizons of Dartmoor – and the choice of going on, ignoring the line to enjoy more of one of the most exciting areas of wild country in Britain, or turning back for further exploration of this fascinating line. Those who turn back can now follow the branch, passed on the way up, that leads to the Haytor quarries. These were never, in fact, a great commercial success, in spite of the immense effort put in to reduce transport costs. Little more than thirty years after the Haytor Tramway was finished, the quarries had closed. Those with no wish to linger over the remnants of a failed enterprise can simply carry on up to the tor itself – and it certainly is an attraction. A great mass of weather-smoothed granite, it rises, clean and bold, out of the surrounding moor. It is a favourite local attraction and, on any day in the summer, it swarms with the young enjoying the fun of clambering to its summit. There is also likely to be a fair representation of the not-

Stony points! A short branch line is led off from the main line of the Haytor Tramway. The stone blocks could not, of course, be moved, so waggons had to be heaved bodily from one track to the other.

so-young, trying to look dignified and pretending that they are not having just as much fun as the children.

From the rock, a gentle walk across the close-cropped grass brings a return to the car park, and a return to the dubious delights of the internal combustion engine, and perhaps the prospect of more real pleasures in the form of refreshment at Haytor Vale. Few of those who come here are aware of the old granite railway, but those who find it are invariably fascinated by it. It is, in many ways, the simplest conceivable system of railways. Yet, at the same time, it shows in the detail of its execution a complete mastery of that intractable granite on which the whole moor rests. It is as much a part of Dartmoor life and history as the roaming bands of ponies, the rocks and the bracken. It is also the finest example we have of a railway constructed without the benefits of iron and steel. It is a last example, for now we are moving not just to iron rails but to the very beginning of the age of the steam locomotive.

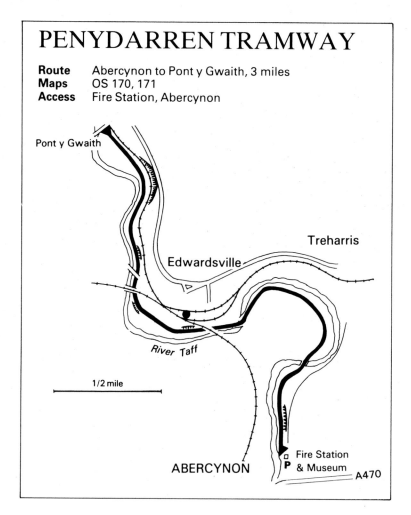

PENYDARREN TRAMWAY

Route   Abercynon to Pont y Gwaith, 3 miles
Maps   OS 170, 171
Access   Fire Station, Abercynon

This is not so much a railway walk as a railway pilgrimage. True, it stands on its own merits as a good example of a typical South Wales tramway, passing through pleasant countryside and still having plenty of physical remains to keep the railway walker's interest high. But what really stirs the blood is the knowledge that it was along this route on 13 February 1804 that, for the very first time, a steam locomotive ran over iron rails. The Cornish engineer, Richard Trevithick, had already secured a considerable reputation as a builder of high-pressure steam engines at a period when Cornwall led the world in such work. At the beginning of the nineteenth century he set about putting his engines on wheels. His first experiments were with road engines and were quite successful until one fateful day when Trevithick and friends spent too long toasting the success of the new venture at a local inn. As they filled up with liquid, the boiler in the engine ran dry, with explosive consequences. By then, however, Trevithick was already planning to put his engines on rails. There is some dispute as to just when and where the first trials were made. There is a possibility that a short run took place at Coalbrookdale, where the parts of the

locomotive were cast and where a plateway was laid. But there is
no doubt that the first full experiment in which the engine hauled a
train of loaded waggons happened here at Penydarren.

The event was partly a genuine industrial experiment and partly
a wager. A local iron master, Samuel Homfray, had a bet of
500 guineas – a very considerable sum indeed – that the new
locomotive could haul a ten-ton load over the 9½ miles of track
between Abercynon and Merthyr Tydfil. There was a general
belief that iron wheels would never grip iron rails, and Homfray's
opponents were sure they were on a winner. As we all know, they
were wrong and Trevithick triumphed. 'It works extremely well . . .',
he wrote after the trial, '. . . and is much more manageable than
horses'. It also tended to fracture the brittle rails and, though the
wager was won, the horses were soon back at Penydarren. But it
was a beginning and it is that beginning that is the lure that draws
many to this area.

If you come into Abercynon from the A470, this road will bring
you to the Fire Station. This stands on the site of the wharf where
the tramway from Merthyr had its southern terminus in a meeting

A tree-shaded lane, a peaceful country scene, where only the massive retaining wall and the line of sleeper blocks give even a hint of a railway past. Yet it is here, on the Penydarren Tramway, that Richard Trevithick made the famous first run with his steam locomotive.

The plaque at Abercynon, commemorating Trevithick's achievement. Mounted on plateway rails set on stone sleeper blocks, it shows the original locomotive.

with the Glamorgan Canal. The whole area has been altered out of all recognition, but a stone tablet has been erected on the site, showing the original engine and including a short length of track mounted on stone blocks. The walk starts here – though the indolent can drive the first section which runs on the narrow road beside the River Taff. In fact, the river is to prove a constant companion throughout the walk, as the tramway follows the extravagant bends of the water course.

The first section was dominated, when I came this way, by the busy traffic of a construction site, where a new, tall bridge was being built across the valley. Inevitably, on such a walk, historic themes emerge and stay at the forefront of the mind. Less than two centuries ago, the horse-drawn waggons of the tramway represented a major technological advance, shortly to be superseded by Trevithick's fire-breathing monster. Yet now the old way is reduced to marks on the ground, while the age of the motor vehicle makes new demands on the skills of civil engineers. Interesting, too, to note that the tramway is reduced to a narrow strip, hugging the river, in contrast to the boldness of the new roadway which appears simply to ignore problems of geography, taking them, literally, in its stride.

The tramway route now swings away behind a row of houses, across the river from Quaker's Yard, and enters a more peaceful stretch. Say 'South Wales' in a word-association test to anyone who has never visited the region and the responses you are likely to get are – pit head, slag heap, and steel. Yet here you have as lovely a river valley as you could hope to find, while the tramway itself is a shady walk, its route overhung by the branches of trees. And all the time, the line is swinging in a great loop where you start off by walking west and end up heading to the east, before turning off to the south over a fine tramway bridge. You could recognize it for what it is by its flat top, but this is not, in fact, a bridge that the famous locomotive ever crossed. In Trevithick's day, the bridges were all of timber but, once locomotives were established on the line, they proved all too inadequate. Their replacement was assured when one finally collapsed under the weight of the lumbering steam horse.

Once across the river, another bridge soon appears, a lofty viaduct rising high above the little tramway – and still in use. What a thrill it would have been for Trevithick had he been able to see that the system he pioneered would advance so far in less than a century – with civil engineering far outstripping anything known in his day and trains working the line, carrying goods of a weight and at a speed that he could scarcely have contemplated. He would perhaps not even have been too dismayed to find, a little further along the way, a second mighty viaduct that had been demolished to make way for a newer form of transport. Trevithick was, after all, a man who looked to the future. There was little hint of sentimentality or nostalgic yearning in his make up.

Now the route becomes scenically even more pleasing and historically more interesting. Lines of stone sleeper blocks become ever more apparent as the tramway carves a route into the steep hillside above the river. The ledge of the track is protected on the upper slope by a stout stone wall, built against the hillside. Just how necessary this is becomes apparent at the few places where the wall has disintegrated, allowing rubble to topple down the hill, earth to wash on to the line to turn the path into a quagmire. Such spots are rare and, on the whole, this is a well-preserved path, threading through the countryside, where sheep easily outnumber the human visitors. Of all the places on the line, this is one where imagination can be given its head. What amazement there must have been among the few shepherds and farmers who saw the sudden emergence of the fiery engine into their placid world. What panic must have spread among the animals, what a twittering of birds and bleating of sheep. And what exhilaration there must have been for the privileged few who rode that first snorting train on its epic journey down the Taff valley.

The 'official' footpath ends at the high, stone bridge across a short cutting, and the walker has already seen the best of the scenery and the best-preserved sections of the old line. It can, however, be followed on northwards and, just south of Merthyr Tydfil, are the tramway tunnels which were filled with smoke and steam in 1804. Those who have seen enough can retrace their steps to Abercynon. And those who have the time might care to take one further excursion to the Welsh Industrial and Maritime Museum at Cardiff, where there is a working replica of the original Trevithick locomotive. But perhaps the greatest appeal of this little walk is that its character is still so very much of the age of horse-drawn traffic, which makes the idea of the sudden emergence of the steam locomotive into such peaceful surroundings seem all the more exciting.

The best-preserved section of the tramway is carved out of the hillside and still has many of its old stone sleeper blocks in place.

HIGH PEAK TRAIL

Route   Cromford Canal to Hurdlow, 17½ miles
Map   OS 119
Access   Black Rocks, off B5036
           Middleton Top, turn west on minor road off B5023
           Middleton Minninglow, minor road south of Pikehall
           on A5012
           Friden, minor road north of junction A5012 and A505
           Parsley Hay, A515
           Hurdlow, south of A515
Cycling Cycle hire at Parsley Hay and Middleton Top
Leaflet Peak National Park and Derbyshire County Council

Opposite Lea Wood Pumping Station at High Peak Junction houses a fine preserved steam engine, originally used to pump water for the Cromford Canal. It marks the beginning of the Cromford and High Peak Railway.

The route follows the Cromford and High Peak Railway, a line that continues the transition from the tramway age into the railway age proper, though its main characteristics are very much those of the earlier times. A nineteenth century author wrote of it as '. . . the skyscraping High Peak Railway with its corkscrew curves that seem to have been laid out by a mad Archimedes endeavouring to square the circle . . .', which certainly does not make it sound like a modern railway. In fact, work began in 1825, the year the Stockton and Darlington Railway was opened, and the line was designed in the best tramway tradition to link two canals, the Cromford and the Peak Forest Canal. The engineer was no deranged mathematician but the highly respected Josias Jessop and he was faced with a route that had to climb to a summit 987 feet (300 metres) above the starting point at Cromford and then drop another 517 feet (157 metres) on the other side. No wonder Jessop was forced to twist and turn and climb towards the sky: but those same problems of geography make this a splendid and unique railway which forms the basis for the longest walk described in this book.

The present route starts at what is erroneously called High Peak Junction beside the Cromford Canal, just over a mile from Cromford. This is, in fact, the site of the old Cromford Goods Yard: High Peak Junction is, not surprisingly, the junction between the C. & H.P.R. and the main Midland Railway line at

The top of the Middleton Incline: the truck stands in front of the engine house, which still contains the pair of beam engines used to haul trains up the steep slope.

the end of a later extension of the route. This extra mile ran beside the canal, past the Lea Wood Pumping Station with its preserved steam engine, which you can see beside the aqueduct. Right from the beginning, this line turns out to be full of interesting locations. On the wharf is the old transit warehouse, where goods were stored to await exchange between railway and canal – and a long-redundant notice still bans steam locomotives from entering the building. The route runs alongside the canal towards Cromford – the work of Josias Jessop lying alongside that of his eminent father, William Jessop, who built the waterway. The next building to be reached is the old maintenance shed, now open to the public. Here you can see film of the railway in its working days, and catch your first sight of the 'fish-bellied' rails originally laid on the line. It is rather tempting to press on towards Cromford itself and the remains of Richard Arkwright's original cotton mill at the end of the canal but, with 17 miles still to go, it is perhaps as well to press on – and upwards.

The line passes beneath the main road and begins the first of its climbs, up the Sheep Pasture incline – three-quarters-of-a-mile long at a gradient that starts at 1 in 9 then steepens to 1 in 8. Haulage was by a continuous rope and steam engine at the top of the hill. You can still see the pulley at the foot of the incline round which the rope was passed. Part way up the line is a hole in the ground, which you might care to pause and contemplate – if only to get a breather. This is a catch pit. In March 1888, two waggons became detached from the rope and hurtled off down the incline. At the bottom where the rails turn sharply towards the wharf, the waggons left the track and soared through the air, crossing both the canal and the main line beyond to smash themselves to pieces in a field. They had covered a distance of some 200 yards (182 metres), the longest recorded flight by a loaded goods waggon! After that the hole was dug, so that any other runaways could be switched on to a track that brought them down into the catch pit. At the top of the incline is the engine house and the track levels out to allow more conventional working.

The next mile or so offers relief from the climb, but there is no lessening of interest. Much of the route is heavily wooded, and a dark and gloomy quarry that might suggest itself as an ideal disposal spot for the murderously inclined adjoins the track. For the non-violent, the quarry is a reminder that stone was one of the principal cargoes carried on the line. The level section is a good place to contemplate the traffic on the railway. At first, everything was horse drawn but, very shortly, the steam locomotive was introduced – and even a passenger line was begun. It was not a very good service, and passengers needed to be pretty fit, for the company made them get out and walk up the inclines. They also had to be patient, for an 1874 timetable shows a train heading out from High Peak Junction at 11.45 am and reaching Whaley Bridge, 30 miles away, at 5.10 pm. But at least they had time to enjoy, as we do still, the splendid views across Cromford to Matlock. You can look across to Willersley Castle, Arkwright's home and to two of his mills, the original and the later Masson Mill – and you can see the latest wonder of the district, the cable car route that spans the gorge. Closer at hand, the Black Rocks stand high above the line. Then the next of the uphill slopes appears, the Middleton Incline rising up towards a massive quarry and the distant outline of the engine house that marks the top.

You can still see traces of stone blocks on the way up the incline and, when you finally reach the top, you are rewarded by what is probably the most exciting site on the entire route – Middleton Top Engine House. A lot of restoration work is still going on here. A waggon sits by the engine house, chained to a length of the old haulage cable; a length of track has been relaid; and – best of all – the engine house still contains its engine. This is a splendid example of a two-cylinder beam engine which dates back to the beginning of the railway in 1825. It is open to the public at weekends, and the good news is that there are plans to get it back into steam – instead of turning it over by compressed air as at present. There are water supply problems, for the old reservoir is now the adjoining cottage garden.

Some of the original fish-bellied rails, mounted on stone blocks and preserved at Middleton Top engine house.

The old maintenance shed has been opened to the public, and films are shown here of the Cromford and High Peak in its working days. The railway itself climbs the hill behind the shed.

There is still a long way to go and it is possible to get off your feet and on to a bike, for cycles can be hired by the day as they can be at Parsley Hay for this and the Tissington Trail. This is certainly a pleasant way of doing the whole route in a day, walking the inclines and cycling the rest. The line still rises, but now at a rather more conventional slope and the scenery takes on the character that will predominate for the remainder of the journey. This is indeed the land of the High Peak, the limestone hills of Derbyshire, and the line is soon to enter the boundaries of the Peak District National Park. It is a country of hill farms, fields divided off by the dry stone walls that straggle, gleaming white on a sunny day, up every slope. It is a land of a few cattle, many more

sheep, and of the quarries that still dot the route. It is a dry land, and one of the jobs of the railway was to bring water to the workings along the way: look out for an upturned locomotive saddle tank along the way which served as a small reservoir for one of the now-abandoned quarries.

We have still not reached the summit; there is one more incline to be faced at Hopton. A short, unlined tunnel brings you out at the foot of the slope, gentle at first at a mere 1 in 60, then steepening in stages – 1 in 30, 1 in 20, and a sharp 1 in 14 at the top. Amazingly, this was worked by conventional locomotives, the steepest gradient to be tackled without the help of cables. The little railway cottages with their Gothicky windows mark the top of

the climb and now, having reached his summit, Jessop was determined to keep his level no matter how many twists and turns he needed to follow the contours of the land – a construction technique common in his father's canal building days. There are few deep cuttings though, in several places, hillside rock had to be blasted out of the way of the line. There are, however, some quite magnificent embankments. It is not merely the height and length of the banks that impress, but their construction, walled and buttressed as though they were the ramparts of some gargantuan castle. They help to give the route its wonderful feeling of airiness, a railway that rides high, offering wide vistas across the surrounding hills and valleys.

Two themes seem to dominate the route: grand views and sheep, the latter rather more than some visitors might wish. The track surface, a compacted black ash that is excellent both for walking and cycling, also acts as a black-body radiator, forming a lovely warm bed for the snoozing animals that prove, not surprisingly, somewhat reluctant to move out of the way. A third theme appears in the form of many mines and quarries along the way. The evidence of mining often appears as little more than disturbances to the evenness of the ground; hollows surrounded by raised rings like landscape doughnuts. The hollows represent collapsed pits, the rings the excavated earth piled around them. The quarries are far more obvious, and one abandoned working near Gotham still has track rusting along its siding, on which an equally decayed and once-mobile crane is parked. Most visitors are unlikely to get overexcited by the evidence of an industrial past and will probably just be content to take in the superb scenery.

Nearing Parsley Hay, the line dives through a short tunnel under the main road. If you look back after you have emerged into the light, you will see a carved emblem above the portal. It shows an early railway waggon, announces that this is the Cromford and High Peak Railway, and then seems uncertain as to who should receive the credit. One inscription, no doubt intended to appeal to down-to-earth, practical men says simply 'Jos^s Jessop Esqr. Engineer', while a second records less plausibly, in Latin, that it was all achieved by the Divine Skill of Pallas. The truth is that it was all achieved by a lot of men with pickaxe, shovel, and black powder – but no-one chose to record their efforts.

Beyond the tunnel there is a junction with the Tissington Trail after which the ways combine to head towards Parsley Hay, the second cycle hire centre. From here, in clear weather, you have a magnificent view right across to the sharp-edged rocks of The Roches, but the end of the line is not far ahead. It comes as something of an anticlimax, the way being barred by active quarry workings close to the point where the original line swung away to Whaley Bridge and a more recent branch led off to Buxton. It is hoped to incorporate an old green way into the trail, so that the route will lead down into the town rather than end somewhat inconclusively in the middle of nowhere. Hardy spirits can, of course, always overcome this slight sense of anticlimax by changing course at Parsley Hay and heading down the Tissington Trail.

Opposite The rocky land-scape of the Peak District offered a very hostile environment to the railway builders, and here at Hopton the stone was blasted away to form a rough cutting culminating in a short tunnel.

TISSINGTON TRAIL

Route Ashbourne to Parsley Hay, Derbyshire, 13 miles
Map OS 119
Access Parsley Hay, A515
Hartington, B5054
Alsop en le Dale, A515
Tissington
Thorpe
Mapleton Lane, Ashbourne
Cycling Cycle hire at Parsley Hay and Ashbourne
Leaflet Peak National Park

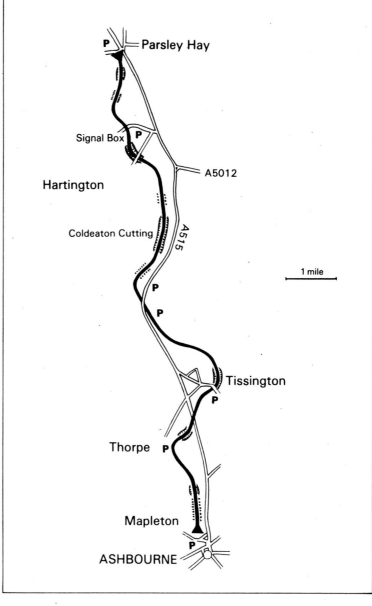

Scenically, the High Peak and Tissington trails have a great deal in common, not too surprising in two lines that make a junction and both run largely within the Peak District National Park. In railway terms, however, they make a complete contrast: the one dating from the very beginning of the steam age, the other from the end, for the Tissington Trail follows the North Western Railway's Ashbourne to Buxton line, opened in 1899. It was one of many late lines which opened with high hopes that remained largely unfulfilled. The promoters, seeing a country rich in natural resources laid plans for a double-track main line, but only succeeded in producing a single-track branch which, measured in financial terms, was something of a flop. In engineering terms, however, it was more of a triumph and, looked at as a line for walkers and cyclists, it is as fine as any in the land.

Those who can organize a one-way trip might like to note that the line rises almost continuously from Ashbourne to Parsley Hay, climbing 650 feet (198 metres) in the course of the journey. So, for this description, I shall assume that all readers share my inherent laziness and will start from the northern end. For the first few hundred metres, the Tissington and the High Peak share common ground out of Parsley Hay, before our present route turns south and at once establishes its separate identity. If the C. & H.P.R. can be characterized by its embankments, then this is a line where the cuttings set the tone. The hill ahead has been carved open, its two halves like an Edam cheese, sliced and separated. There is scarcely time to enjoy the hill scenery before you are plunged into the rocky rift. Today, it seems almost to be a natural feature, for plant life has burgeoned on the steep slopes of the cutting, sheep graze, and even a few trees have found a home on the rim. Yet once it must have been a glaring scar on the land. Did anyone protest at this ravaging of the landscape? It seems unlikely, and now the old scar has become a feature to be preserved.

Coming out of the cutting you enter on to what is certainly my favourite section of the line. It bends round in a great s to make its way between the hills in a landscape which contrives to hold simultaneously a cosy domesticity and a touch of dangerous wildness. The hills, latticed with stone walls and green lanes, dotted by sheep, and open to the elements offer an environment which many might consider harsh – and come this way in winter and you will discover just how harsh it can be. But the hill farms, sheltered and snug in their hollows, sending up plumes of grey smoke from their chimneys, promise only comfort and warmth. Between these two worlds goes the line, heading on towards one of the few preserved railway buildings, the signal box, clean and smart, its levers oiled ready for use – but there are now no signals to pull, no points to change. Hartington Station, from which they used to send milk up to London, not to mention the locally produced Stilton cheeses, has vanished as well. The line too does a vanishing act, disappearing into yet another cutting beneath the shadow of quarry spoil heaps.

Coming out of the cutting into the open, the details of the scene may have changed, but not the essential qualities. Across the fields

Shortly after leaving the junction with the High Peak Trail, the walker on the Tissington Trail is faced by this spectacular cutting.

is the distant settlement of Biggin, the square church tower announcing its presence. Because the early settlers had no thoughts of railways in mind when they established their villages, they seldom placed them in a spot that any railway would ever reach. The route of the line is dictated by the lie of the land not the presence of habitation, so that most villages are merely glimpsed but not encountered. Ahead now the land seems especially daunting for railway builders, a long, low range of hillocks barring the way. The early engineers, such as Jessop on the High Peak, would have thought of all kinds of ingenious ways of overcoming the obstacles, but half a century later the problem was simply met head on. Johnson's Hillock – and, incidentally what was it about Mr Johnson that made him so awkward, for he has another hillock set right in the path of the Leeds and Liverpool Canal some miles to the north? – stands as the most prominent feature, a rounded hill with a crown of trees. Below it, the line was pushed ahead in a deep cutting, 60 feet (18 metres) below the surface at one point, and three-quarters-of-a-mile long. In places you can still see the shattered rock but, elsewhere as with the other cuttings, grass has blurred the edges. Vast amounts of stone were shifted to make a way through the hill. Where did it all go? Something of an answer appears when you emerge on the far side.

I was lucky when I came this way to find a specialist at work, restoring the dry stone walls that separate the adjoining fields. I stopped for a chat, and it was he who pointed out that the railway, too, had its own boundary walls and he also passed on the information that, to his knowledge, the stone walls we see today are precisely those walls which were built when the line was new, the best part of a century ago. The walls were, he said, in first-class condition, a tribute not just to their builders but to the durability of this traditional style of construction which does so much to determine the visual make up of the Pennine landscape. He also looked back over a lifetime spent in the region and on the many times he had travelled the line, both in the comfort of summer and in winter when the going could get really hard. As he reminisced, I could picture the scene of snow-covered hills and iced rails, with a little locomotive, its fire burning fiercely before the sweating fireman, the driver trying to coax it forward as its wheel slipped in spite of continuous sanding. At least, they would have been able to look forward to an easier passage on the downhill trips.

The line now comes close to the main Ashbourne-Buxton road, and it is interesting to note how much easier life was for road engineers than for those who designed the railways. The road goes up hill and down dale with very little concern for gradients, charging up slopes that would utterly defeat any locomotive. So, the two soon part company again, the road heading straight for its destination, the railway swinging off on yet another curl around the hills. This is no longer the hard, almost bare, country of the northern section. It is still hilly, but now the hills are smoother and grassier, dotted with copses. But the farms still have that same close-clenched feel of their neighbours, crouched in the lee of the land, centre points of a web of stone walls. Just look at Shaw Farm to the north of the line – a perfect example.

Beyond this, the line actually makes contact, for once, with a village – Tissington, which gives the trail its name. It is a rather polite-looking place, very much an estate village, but famous for its well dressing. There are four wells in the village and each year they are decorated by Biblical scenes composed out of thousands of flowers. Tissington also marks the beginning of the rather more domesticated section of the line. Beyond the village, the land begins to even out its bumps, farms become more frequent and take on more of a lowland character. Not that the other

The magnificent country-side of the Derbyshire hills, with the farmhouse sitting comfortably in the centre of a web of dry stone walls. The photograph was taken from the Tissington Trail, which curves round above the valley to disappear into the deep cutting, visible at the top of the picture.

Derbyshire is ever far away. Another swing across the main road brings you to Thorpe – or rather Thorpe's pub – and Thorpe sits at the entrance to Dovedale. Goodness knows how many tourists turn up every year to enjoy the scenery, tripping over one another's feet, remarking how splendid it is to get away from it all. Yet this old railway, if it cannot quite match the drama of Dovedale, offers pleasures as profound – and far fewer people. From the line you can look down on the narrow roads, blocked with cars and coaches and give thanks that they are not going your way!

For the rest of the way, the trail changes character yet again, offering a secluded, tree-lined track on high banks that look out over wide tracts of country. Rather surprisingly, a farm of red brick appears in the midst of this essentially stony country, not that it is anything other than handsome but it does seem an anachronism. Ahead, the tall spire of Ashbourne church announces the end of the line. You can return on foot, or catch a bus back to Parsley Hay, getting tantalizingly brief glimpses of the trail as you go. Cyclists, however, might like to contemplate a third option. From Ashbourne to Wirksworth is only 9 miles by road and there you can join the High Peak and follow that back to Parsley Hay, combining the two lines in one round trip. Whichever way you choose, you will find the combination of superb scenery and fascinating railway history hard to beat.

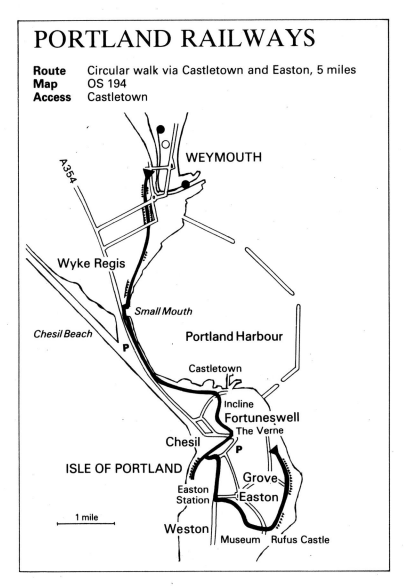

PORTLAND RAILWAYS

Route   Circular walk via Castletown and Easton, 5 miles
Map   OS 194
Access   Castletown

WEYMOUTH

A354

Wyke Regis

Small Mouth

Chesil Beach

Portland Harbour

P

Castletown

Incline
Fortuneswell
The Verne

Chesil

P

ISLE OF PORTLAND

Grove
Easton

Easton
Station

1 mile

Weston

Museum   Rufus Castle

Portland was, in effect, an island until 1839, when the first bridge was built joining it to the mainland. There was a tenuous link before that via the shifting stones of Chesil Beach, but it was the bridge that made for easy movement between Portland and the rest of the world – not an event universally welcomed among the islanders, who were not especially fond of strangers. Portlanders were, in fact, known as 'slingers', from their somewhat antisocial habit of slinging rocks at anyone they did not know – though whether this was from a general dislike of foreigners or the suspicion that the stranger might be an Excise man out to stop the favourite island pastime of smuggling is uncertain. In railway terms, Portland remained an island somewhat longer, until 1865 when the first train chugged across the new viaduct at Wyke Regis. It was from the first a curious affair, being operated jointly by the

Great Western and London and South Western Railways, so that it was laid as broad gauge, with a standard-gauge track inside that.

You can still walk much of the line between Weymouth and the terminus at Easton, but not all of it, for this has never been made into an official walkway. To many people it seemed madness to close this most scenic of railways in the first place – think what a successful preserved line it would have made, running out of the popular resort of Weymouth. Having closed it, it now seems equally sad that the authorities have not taken the opportunity to use the trackbed as a footpath, but now alas much has been lost. You can start in Weymouth itself by the old station, next to the present British Rail station, and follow the route through the tidy villas, past Sandsfoot Castle looking slightly incongruous in its neat, municipal park, but, at Wyke Regis, you are faced with a gap where the viaduct used to be. You can take to the road and follow the line across the causeway and on to the island, only to lose it again at the guarded gates of the naval base. But that disappointment turns out to be only a minor irritation, for now you can set about the true enjoyment of the Portland railways and turn to a route that was built in the days when this was still an island – the Merchants' Railway.

Portland has always provided its own major industry out of its own fabric, the stone of which the island is composed. Christopher Wren came here to choose the stone for St Paul's, and many others have followed him. But the islanders were faced with immense problems in moving the stone from quarry to harbour. The Reverend J Skinner, visiting the area in 1804, wrote of the stone waggons hitched up for downhill runs with one horse in front and two behind. It was the horses to the rear that took the most punishment: '. . . they squat down on their haunches and suffer themselves to be dragged for many yards, struggling with all their strength against the weight that forces them forwards. To one unaccustomed to the sight, it appears as though their limbs must inevitably be dislocated, or their sinews cracked by the violence of their exertions: indeed one compassionates these poor creatures, the rather, as all this labour might easily be obviated by the simple construction of a rail road.' It was not, in fact, to be long before the rail road was provided, for work began on it in 1825. The Merchants' Railway was a tramway, very like, in its essentials, the Cromford and High Peak, but it is unusual in that so much of its original tramway character has been preserved.

The route starts close by the old castle at Castletown, as the point where the stone was loaded at the quayside. Here a long incline, Freeman's Incline, runs straight up the hill, passing under the later railway bridge of the Weymouth-Portland line. You only have to walk up a little way before you receive confirmation that you are indeed on the right track, for those unmistakable stone blocks are still exposed on the hillside. This was a self-acting incline. Because virtually all the traffic was from quarry to quay, the weight of the descending, loaded trucks could be used to lift the empty trucks back up the hill. It is a long plod up the hill, but you are rewarded by increasingly fine views over Chesil beach and the Dorset coast.

Opposite The Merchants' Railway runs across the deep cleft below the Verne, the route dividing between the top pair of bridges. It is a happy reminder that, even before the railway age proper had begun, engineers were able to cope with major construction problems.

After pausing for breath at the top of the slope, you will find the track easy to follow through a smart, new stone bridge under the road. It then divides into upper and lower routes that follow more-or-less parallel lines in a great U-curve around the steep hillside. The twin tracks allowed two-way working on the line as it heads off towards the quarries. The route passes beneath the Verne, the old citadel of Portland, designed originally to keep people out, but now used to keep them in, for it has been turned into the Portland prison. At the Verne, the complex of routes passes over a fine series of bridges, but the main line is easily followed as it passes the popular viewpoint below the Portland Heights Motel, and then crosses the main road. Here it breaks up into a whole series of branches, each heading towards one of the ancient quarries. There is a maze to explore here, as a complex of paths twists round the blocks of stone, still bearing the marks of the quarrymen. Among them are newer markings, for the quarries had a brief flowering as a sculpture park. One more handsome bridge appears, inscribed J C Lano 1854. Very important people the Lanos in this part of the world – their monuments dominate the churchyard of St George's.

Once you have finished exploring the various routes around the quarries, you can return to the road and walk south down Wide Street – though, after the incline, you might feel moved towards the George Inn, an ancient building where the Court Leet, showing great good sense, used to hold their meetings. True stalwarts can march briskly on up Reforme to the site of the old Easton Railway Station. Not much now remains – even the famous fossil ammonites that used to grace the station wall have gone. But the more modern line is no more difficult to follow than its predecessor. It too threads between quarries, in a deep cutting, before it reaches the main road out to Portland Bill. The track under the road is frequently waterlogged, so that it is usually easier to clamber up to road level for the crossing, where you will find the little museum which houses many relics of Portland's past – including the railway past. It is well worth a visit.

The line now becomes temporarily a little difficult to follow because, since the closure, the quarrymen have bulldozed parts of the scenery into new shapes. The simplest way is to take the track between that heading to the quarry complex and that heading for the genuine ruins of Rufus Castle and the mock embattlements of Pennsylvania Castle. Follow the cliff above Church Ope and you will reach a newly bulldozed path leading down to the unmistakable wide ledge of the railway. This part of the journey emphasizes the problems that can be met in walking 'unofficial' railway paths. I have been coming to the area for many years but, on the most recent occasion, I became quite confused, and it was only when I heard that the bulldozers had yet again rearranged the landscape just a week before that all became clear. So, be warned – the description I have just given may not be a description of the landscape that you will find. The excursion has its difficulties – but the rewards are immense, for the line around the eastern cliffs is as splendid as any you will find in Britain. It shoulders right up to the white cliffs as it begins its slow, curving descent back down to

Opposite The dramatic setting of the railway above the East Weare on Portland. An immense labour was involved in blasting the track through the stone of the cliffs, and shattered fragments from the blasting still clutter the valley sides.

The whole island of Portland is still dotted with reminders of its importance as a source of building stone, blocks such as this were cut for the building of St Paul's in London.

Castletown. The area beneath the cliffs is known as the East Weare, a wilderness of overgrown boulders – and much of that wilderness was created by the stone shoved aside to make way for the railway. There is one further impediment to progress, in the form of the rifle range. A red flag flies on firing days and restrictions cover movement in the area. You can, in any case, turn back to the path along the Weare. It is a dramatic and, in human terms, lonely stretch of coast – but in other ways it is a busy, noisy spot. Seabirds of all kinds congregate here – and it only needs one gull to start squawking for the rest to set up in opposition, rather like an ornithological debate in Parliament, with no-one to call order. Out at sea, the fishing boats scurry around the coast, while further out there are occasional sightings of the ferry out of Weymouth or something less peaceful from the naval base. What a loss this line has proved to be. As you retrace your steps towards Easton, you can only contemplate what might have been – or, in my wife's case, what was for she had the good fortune to travel this line while the trains still ran. I envy her the experience, and console myself with the thought that Portland still provides a chance to explore two very different but equally fascinating railway walks.

TALYLLYN RAILWAY

Route   Nant Gwernol to Bryneglwys, 3-mile circular walk
Map   OS 124
Access Road access, Tywyn Wharf Station and Abergynolwyn
         Station

A word first about access: those who wish to eschew the delights of
a steam railway and prefer to travel by car and by foot must go to
Abergynolwyn Station and follow the waymarked route to Nant
Gwernol, which cannot be reached by road. But this walk is really
intended for those enthusiasts who want to combine railway past
and railway present in one glorious expedition. For them, the
route starts at Tywyn and the wait for the morning train on the
Talyllyn Railway. As this is an account of a walk rather than a
train journey there will be only the briefest description of the
delights to be enjoyed by those who travel the rails from Tywyn to
Nant Gwernol, but some words about the railway are necessary for
the walk is on the same line, reaching, as the adverts say, those
parts that the train cannot reach.

The story begins in 1847, when slate mining began at Bryn
Eglwys, high in the hills above Tywyn. There was a long, difficult
journey to bring the slate down to the waiting ships at Aberdovey
and it might have remained a long, difficult journey but for the
American Civil War. That war brought a cotton famine to
Lancashire and the local manufacturers looked for alternative
investments – and they looked over to North Wales and the rapidly
expanding slate industry. So, Manchester money went into

building a railway to the quarries, not from Aberdovey, but from a new port at Tywyn. It was built as a narrow-gauge line and has a special place in the affection of all lovers of steam, for it was the first railway to be taken over and run by volunteers. Today you can travel the line, possibly hauled by *Dolgoch*, a locomotive that was delivered brand new to the Talyllyn when the line opened in 1866. The little train climbs steadily up the side of the hill, with the scenery becoming progressively grander. It crosses above the Dolgoch Falls on a tall viaduct, then swings round at Abergynolwyn towards Nant Gwernol. And, all the time, the little engine is beating away, working hard throughout the climb.

Nant Gwernol was always the end of the line for steam traction, but it was never the end of the railway – and the walk will take us to the end of the line, the quarries of Bryn Eglwys. Below the station is the busy, tumbling river that gives the place its name and, at the end of the rails, paths diverge. To the left, waymarked yellow, green, and blue, three walks entice you on a pleasant level stroll through the woods to the river. None of these is our path. We take the alternative way, straight up the hillside on a narrow path. This is the other part of the Talyllyn, the tramway section of cable-worked inclines and level sections where horses pulled the trucks of slate. Indeed, you can still see the old, rusting cable snaking down the hill beside the path. This is the Alltwyllt Incline – a name only a native-born Welshman should attempt to pronounce – and it comes in two parts. At the end of the first, another level path appears to tempt you away, but your route lies up the even steeper second half of the incline. A good deal of restoration work has gone on at the top. A length of track has been laid so that, standing at the top, you can see the rails running along then suddenly plunging over the edge, like a fairground roller coaster. Set high in the rocks above is the cable drum, which was controlled by a brake lever which was positioned to allow the brakeman to see down the slope. As at Portland, this was a self-acting incline.

At the top of the incline there are also the ruins of a small building which was the stable for the horses that worked the next section, which most walkers are relieved to find is a flat ledge cut into the hill. Enclosed by trees, there is very little impression of height, until you realize that what you are seeing on the downhill side of the tracks are not tiny trees, but the tops of very tall trees growing in the precipitous bank. The walk hugs the hill and there are many reminders of the railway past in the shape of old sleepers and even the remains of a typical slate waggon. The path now reaches the river which, at this height, is little more than a wide stream. A wooden footbridge leads across to one of the official forest walks, while another path climbs through the woods above the stream, but this is where the intrepid must depart from the official way, if the actual tramway route is to be followed. At the point where the forest path begins to zig-zag up the hill, look across the stream and you will see the abutments of the tramway bridge and beyond that the built-up stone sides of the Cantrybedd Incline. It is an easy matter to hop over the stream and clamber up on to the incline. It is another steep, and rather rough, climb, but

Opposite The little loco-motive *Sir Haydn*, built in 1878, pauses at Nant Gwernol before running round its train for the return journey to Tywyn. The railway walk starts up along the incline to the right of the engine, and ends on the path to the left.

it brings you out, at last, at the hill-top quarries.

Here, promontories of shattered slate provide viewing platforms, from which you can look down the deep, green vee of the tree-filled valley and across to the distant hills. This is the start of that system that, over the years, sent 300 000 tons of slate down the railway to roof the houses of Britain. Now all is dereliction. Until very recently, there were extensive remains of buildings, but now they have been demolished to add their share to the rubble on the hill top. The tramway, however, continues, its path marked by a low slate wall, to a small river and another demolished bridge, where unsupported rails stick forlornly from the bank. It is possible to cross the stream and continue on to the upper quarry level, reached by the last of the inclines, though here again, there has been considerable demolition in recent years. It seems strange to look around now and think that not so long ago some 300 men worked here every day.

Those who are beginning to get a little anxious about train times – and it will prove a long day's walk if you miss the last train home – can turn from the last bridge on to the broad, forest road which, though it appears to head off in the wrong direction, doubles back on itself to head again towards the river. Shortly after the u-turn, a white post indicates the beginning of the footpath that provides a

delightful way through the woods to the foot of the Cantrybedd
Incline. You can now retrace your steps along the tramway, but I
would recommend taking the alternative route across the footbridge. This follows the cascading river, but also gives an
opportunity to see the way in which the tramway track across the
valley is built up above stone walls that buttress it against land slip.
A second footbridge leads back to Nant Gwernol station, but just
take a look at the river near the foot of the incline. Fragments of
timber and chunks of rusted metal tell of the fate of those trucks
that broke from the cable and raced down the incline to end in the
river.

How far you walk on this excursion will depend on how
energetic you feel – and on the train timetable. If you have time to
spare, you can follow the waymarked route on to Abergwynolwyn,
where tea and buns are dispensed at the station buffet. Or you can
simply sit and wait for the chuff and whistle of the train, watch as
the tiny engine runs round the coaches to get back to the right
position for the return trip, and take your place in the train. And,
back at Tywyn, it is worth spending a little extra time at the
excellent Narrow Gauge Museum at the station. It makes a
fascinating end to a day that uniquely combines the delights of
steam travel and railway walking.

The top of the Alltwyllt
Incline above Nant Gwernol.
The rails drive over the top
for all the world like a fairground rollercoaster.

WASKERLEY WAY AND DERWENT WALK

Waskerley Way
Route   Meeting Slacks to Consett, 7 miles
Maps   OS 87, 88
Access   Meeting Slacks, on minor road to Waskerley, off B6278
              Waskerley
Cycling
Leaflet Durham County Council
Derwent Walk
Route   Shotley Bridge to Swalwell, Durham, 10 miles
Map   OS 88
Access   Shotley Bridge on B6310
              Ebchester on B6309
              Rowlands Gill on B6314
Cycling
Leaflet Durham County Council

Map showing WASKERLEY WAY and DERWENT WALK with locations: CONSETT, Derwent Walk, Lanchester, Valley Walk, Swalwell, Castleside, Hownes Gill Viaduct, Coke Works, Rowley Station, Whitehall, route of incline, Meeting Slacks, Nanny Mayors Incline, Paddock Hill, Rowlands Gill, A694, Viaduct, Waskerley, Burnhill Junction, Derwentcote, Lintz Green Viaduct, Hamsterley Viaduct, Longclose Bank, Ebchester, DERWENT WALK, Shotley Bridge, CONSETT. Scale: 1 mile

Opposite Meeting Slacks on the Waskerley Way: the line of the old tramway section can be seen heading off across the moors. The stones that mark the edge of the car park are old sleeper blocks.

When first planning this trip it was my intention to include just the one walk, but the appeal of combining two such very different railways into a single route proved irresistible. It provides an ideal opportunity to produce one of those 'compare and contrast' exercises so beloved of examining boards.

In many respects, the Waskerley Way is reminiscent of other routes we have looked at, particularly the Cromford and High

An embankment on the Derwent Valley Walk still carries the lone reminder that the route being walked today was once a part of the London and North Eastern Railway empire.

Peak. It began as a tramway through difficult country with inclines and horse-drawn waggons, and survived, in modified form, into the steam locomotive age. Opened in 1833, the Stanhope and Tyne Railway was very much a mineral line, designed to bring the limestone, lead, and iron of Weardale to the port of South Shields. Those who approach by car from the south along the B6278 will soon see the first of the inclines running alongside the road out of Stanhope, with the remains of winding engine houses at top and bottom. The Weatherhill engine that occupied the top engine house can be seen in the National Railway Museum at York, and it is a splendid example, showing the robust character of these early steam engines. After some eighty years of use it was replaced in 1919 by a more modern, but not it would seem a more efficient, engine. The replacement broke down and the veteran had to be pressed back into service, which says a good deal about the quality of Victorian engineering. Road and rail part company temporarily until the motorist turns right and, at Meeting Slacks, where there was once another engine and another incline, the trail proper is joined.

The line shoots off down the hill towards Waskerley, a quiet little village these days, but once a bustling rail centre. In 1858, the Stockton and Darlington Railway Company became involved in the area and, by constructing the viaduct we shall cross later, opened the way for locomotives to reach this remote moorland. Waskerley, 1150 feet (350 metres) above sea level, became the unlikely setting for a railway town. It is hard to imagine now: the village has shrunk, the shops have closed; the goods station, the shed for six engines, and the sidings have all gone. What remains is the splendid scenery, the exhilaration of walking through a wild landscape, where the few trees bend and arch their backs to the wind.

Originally, the route went north-east down another incline, named after Nanny Mayor who kept the local alehouse. The coming of the locomotive involved a major realignment, with extensive engineering works. The new route swings south, part of the work put in by the S. & D.R., to Burnhill Junction. This is, in effect, the Waskerley branch, joining the main line from Darlington. The route turns through nearly 360 degrees to head north again through a deep cutting blasted through the hillside, its rocky slopes and steep sides giving some indication of the vast amount of labour that went into its construction. It is worth noting, in passing, that the line marked on the Ordnance Survey map as the Waskerley Way is, in fact, the old line and not the recommended pathway. After the wilderness, comes a touch of civilization, as the line reaches, but scarcely touches, Rowley. Rowley Station still exists and steam trains still stop there – but not here. The whole thing was dismantled and re-erected at the North of England Open Air Museum at Beamish.

A mile beyond the station lies the great obstacle that defeated the early engineers, the deep cleft of Hownes Gill. First they tried inclines up and down the valley sides, but they could only take one truck at a time. This was followed by a funicular, which was very little better, and that lasted until the S. & D.R. appeared with the

The Hamsterley viaduct rears up above the woods that fill the valley floor. It is this and the other viaducts along the way that give this walk its unique high-level character.

obvious answer – a viaduct. And you can see why the early engineers were deterred, for it really is a monster, standing a full 150 feet (45 metres) above the valley floor. From it, the walker looks down on the tree tops of the wooded slopes of hills which are, in fact, nothing more than overgrown spoil heaps, for we are now on the edge of the once mighty steel town of Consett. Ahead, the cliffs rise up, great mountains of slag, but they will rise no further. The works have died and much of Consett died with them.

Consett is the meeting point for three railway walks – the Waskerley we have just travelled, the Lanchester Valley which turns south, and the Derwent Valley we are about to follow. It starts by heading off through the town, before turning more to the east towards the Tyne. This old North Eastern Railway branch line is most aptly named after the Derwent, for the river really determines the nature of the line. It was opened in 1867, a time when engineers were in no mood to be deflected from their chosen path by a river, not even a large one. So, within 11 miles there are no fewer than four grand viaducts over the river and its tributaries. None of this is immediately apparent, for the first part of the walk involves a high-level passage round a hill before the valley itself is reached. It follows a somewhat sinuous path, keeping to the contours as far as possible, but occasionally having to take a slice through rising ground. These cuttings may obliterate the wider vistas, but they also serve to cut out the distant hum from the main road which also occupies the narrow valley rather as if one was presented with instant double glazing. At Ebchester, still high up on the hillside, the little signal cabin has been retained as an information centre – and, for those suffering from pangs of thirst, a large pub stands immediately above the line. Now the line begins to turn, swaying off towards the woods around Hamsterley.

It is easy enough here to forget that this was an industrial region and we are walking an industrial line but, in fact, in these Hamsterley Woods, you can find evidence of steel making as far back as the eighteenth century. The area was ideal, with its supplies of iron ore and wood for the furnace fuel, charcoal, and it was here that a crude form of steel, blister steel, was made. The remains of one of the old furnaces can be seen in the woods beyond the main road (OS map reference 131565). For those unattracted by crumbling furnace remains, there are delights ahead to be enjoyed without the need to stray one metre from the line, starting with the 120-foot (36-metre) high, 600-foot (182-metre) long Hamsterley viaduct. Walking the line here is a rather curious experience, for you start with a backdoor view of the rather smart commuter suburb of Hamsterley Mill before you emerge quite suddenly on to the viaduct and a view of a quite different world. Here are the buildings, including the mill itself, of a former age, all half lost in the thickly wooded valley. Pausing for a while on the viaduct, I found myself watching the home life of the birds from a new perspective, looking down on them, rather than up at them, as they busied themselves among the tree tops in a flurry of house building. Hamsterley viaduct has scarcely passed before the Lintz Green viaduct appears, not quite so impressive as its neighbour, but a grand structure nonetheless.

After the excitement of the viaducts, there is a somewhat calmer section, where the view is of crops and pasture and the ruins are not of industry but of the little Friarside Chapel, one of the many victims of Henry VIII's blitz on all monastic foundations. It stands now, a lonely shell among the fields on the outskirts of Rowlands Gill. This is one of the many similar settlements that owe their being to the coming of the railways, which enabled city workers to toil in the town but live in the country. It also provides the next rail spectacular, viaduct number three and indeed a glimpse of viaduct number four in the distance. Here, there is easy access to the valley floor, where the viaduct can be viewed in its river setting. Nearby, too, is Gibside Chapel, a very grand eighteenth-century mausoleum, built in the Palladian style and now owned by the National Trust. The ruins of the hall itself can also be seen from the walk, while the 140-foot (43-metre) high column of the Gibside monument is virtually inescapable. The railway, too, has its moment of glory, with what is perhaps the most impressive section of sustained engineering effort on the whole line. It dips into the lovely mixed woodland of Paddock Wood in a half-mile long cutting, that reaches a depth of 60 feet (18 metres), before emerging into the open for the final crossing of the Derwent on the last of the viaducts. Here the two faces of this stretch of country can be seen together: look south and you see the romantic ruins of Old Hollinside, a thirteenth-century fortified house; turn north and you are faced by the grassed but still unmistakable hump of a colliery spoil heap. The heap, however, offers one bonus: for it follows that if you have a clear view of the heap from the viaduct, then you must get a good view of the viaduct from the heap.

For the rest of the journey it is the world of collieries that dominates the scene. Even the riches of Axwell Hall, glimpsed

Opposite The splendid Hownes Gill viaduct that carries the Waskerley Way 150 feet (45 metres) above the valley floor. It is hard to believe that just ahead lies the once-mighty steel town of Consett.

across the river, were paid for by the wealth hard won underground. This is still an area where the coal industry is active and the Derwenthaugh coke works quite dominates the landscape, a dark bulk rising up from the valley floor and occasionally belching up great clouds of smoke and steam like a snorting dragon. The route ends in theory at the Swalwell Station site but, on my visit, everything was obscured by the work of building contractors. Only the rugby club proudly proclaimed the name of 'Blaydon', but no-one was playing, nor was there any sign of races. Blaydon seems a world away from the moors and Waskerley, yet the two places are joined by more than just an old railway connection and a walk, for both owed their existence to the minerals beneath the ground – to lead, coal, and iron – and to the industries that grew around them. And for the walker, there is another unifying theme, for both the Waskerley Way and the Derwent Valley Walk prove that it is possible to travel through an area that has existed for centuries on industry and yet find peace and beauty.

The lonely moorland section of the Waskerley Way, near the village of Waskerley itself.

WEAVERS' WAY

Route	Blickling to Stalham, 15 miles
Map	OS 133
Access	Blickling Hall
	Felmingham Station
	North Walsham, off B1145
	Honing Station
	Bengate, south of A149
	Stalham, in main street by A149
Leaflet	Norfolk County Council

Opposite Walkers out enjoying early spring weather on the Weavers' Way. This is a line which offers quiet rural pleasures, rather than the drama of great viaducts, cuttings, and embankments.

So far, we have been looking at routes which, in one way or another, close the gap between the tramway age and the age of steam railways. Now we are very much into the latter and, as far as walks are concerned, we have reached the abandoned line par excellence – the old branch line. And, to start us off, here is a line which really does have all the charm and attraction that one expects from such routes. It was a part of the line laid down by the Midland and Great Northern Railways to join Kings Lynn to Yarmouth with, it would appear, stations at every village and hamlet along the way. Perhaps, strictly speaking, this is not a branch line at all, because the multitude of small companies that amalgamated to form the M. & G.N.R. no doubt each saw their own concerns as rivalling in importance the mightiest in the land. But, because the line was single track and as the main towns along the way all had other, and far grander, connections, whatever the high and exalted ambitions of the railway promoters might have been, a branch line it became and as a branch line it died.

The walk itself is not entirely limited to railway tracks, as parts have disappeared beneath modern roads, but the railway occupies by far the larger part. It is a line which can be joined at either end or at various points between but, for those following the whole route, there are two basic choices: start at Blickling Hall in a blaze

The old railway may have died but here beside the Weavers' Way is evidence that its usefulness has not yet ended. A local farmer has converted a disused freight waggon into a small barn.

of Jacobean glory and end at Stalham opposite the chip shop – or go the other way. The advantages of the former are that the route is slightly easier to follow and, at a little over half distance, North Walsingham offers a lunch stop and the comforting knowledge that you are well on your way. To reverse the process is to build up towards the grand climax of architectural splendour. Railway enthusiasts, however, tend to regard Jacobean mansions as North Staffordshire railway stations with delusions of grandeur, so as we have to start somewhere, we shall start at Blickling and set off on our way to the chippie.

The walk begins here precisely because the hall is here and there are car parking facilities; consequently, the first mile of the way is by minor road and path until the railway is reached. It certainly offers an attractive introduction to the walk, and those who care deeply for English architecture may find the lure of Blickling Hall and nearby Old Hall all but irresistible, and never get on to the walk at all. Those who resist temptation will find the railway has a gentle beginning as it curves gently round the north side of Aylsham and across the River Bure. Aylsham itself issues a siren call to come and linger for it is among the most delightful of Norfolk towns, full of excellent flint buildings. That this is the obvious material to use for construction in this part of the world is very evident to anyone walking the line, for flint nodules abound among the ballast that still remains – in a few places in such quantity as to make walking a touch hard on the feet. It is worth casting more than a cursory glance over these flint buildings, for many have fascinating details – look out, for example, for those where the flints have been used to pick out dates and initials on the walls. Aylsham is a town where the many grand buildings provide evidence of prosperity, and the source of that prosperity has given our walk its name. For here we are in the heart of the old East Anglia to which the woollen and linen industries were brought from Holland and Belgium in medieval times, and the influence of those regions can still be seen in the many gabled buildings met with along the way. Certainly the railway builders would have been hard put to it to match this architectural richness and, perhaps wisely, they did not try. Styles are plain but honest, and none the worse for that.

At the last of the Aylsham bridges, the railway is temporarily lost and walkers turn up the road to the north, then along a green lane that takes them to the by-pass where they regain the railway, which is followed to North Walsham. Diversion and railway meet beside the old level-crossing house, now sadly marooned amid a sea of scrap. The house, however, still displays its old railway number cast into the wall. Now the true nature of this walk begins to assert itself.

'Very flat, Norfolk', wrote Noel Coward: well, flat yes, but not very flat. The land heaves itself up in a series of steady undulations, for which the engineers were forced to compensate by low banks and shallow cuttings: nothing ambitious, but enough to provide variety. Certainly, the overall impression is of a flat, wide land beneath big skies, of a very English landscape of ploughed fields and coppices. It is dotted with farms, and the villages proclaim their presences by tall church towers. These latter are again marks of the prosperity of old textile Norfolk, for the churches of the area are of a size and magnificence that seem out of all proportion to their modern setting. The recurring towers provide reference points and markers throughout the journey. Not that one needs to keep one's eyes on distant horizons, for there is plenty of interest nearer at hand. Coming this way in early spring the railway blooms with daffodils along the banks and primroses find a home among the ballast. The sandy soil is much to the liking of the local rabbits, and a Jack Russell that had joined us for the walk as unofficial guide, found the rabbits much to his liking. It is a remarkably tranquil region, apart from the occasional noisy eruptions of bird scarers and passing jet fighters.

Stations make regular appearances, starting with Felmingham and its long, long platform – how many passengers were they expecting? Whatever the hopes, there will be no more trains here now, nor goods waggons in the sidings. They have all gone but, if you look over the neatly balustraded bridge at the nearby farm, you can see where some at least of those waggons ended their days. Now the line disappears into woodland, genuine old mixed woodland, not the dull conifers of more modern plantations. There is a promise of sport in Perch Lake Plantation; marsh marigolds bloom by a stream and primroses thrive in the shade.

The line continues, its sides bordered by trees to the outskirts of North Walsham, where it does another of its disappearing acts. The town may lack the more obvious charms of Aylsham, but it makes a very welcome lunch stop. Beer drinkers who remember

A distance post records the mileage for train drivers who will never come this way again.

Aylsham encourages the walker to pause for a while to enjoy such fine sights as the old mill, sitting above the calm waters of the mill pond.

Norfolk in the not-too-distant past as a real ale desert will be happy to know that this is no longer the case. Adnams has colonized the region from its base in Suffolk to spread contentment through the land, and reinforce the traveller for the next stage. The way out of North Walsham is well sign posted, which is just as well, for the railway is still nowhere to be seen and the Weavers' Way takes a complex path. Take the Yarmouth road out of town; then, at the edge of the built-up area, turn left into Thirlby Road and continue along the pathway over the fields to the minor road. Turn left down the road, right at the junction, and right again into Holgate Lane. Then a left turn and a right turn bring you to Bengate. Those who are already too bewildered to attempt this can simply follow the by-pass which is, in any case, the line of the railway. At Bengate, the railway walk is rejoined with much relief.

Those who try to follow the official leaflet should now ignore the indicated detour, for that was made when no bridge crossed the canal. That omission has been rectified and a new and rather handsome timber bridge now spans the waterway, enabling you to keep on the track to journey's end at Stalham. Canal and railway now remain as close companions for quite some way. The former is the North Walsham and Dilham Canal which passed into transport history long before the last train ran. Perhaps the canal will itself be restored one day, and those interested in such matters might like to pause to glance at the remains of a lock just south of

the railway. Here, too, is another candidate for restoration in the form of a tower windmill, now sail-less.

Beyond the canal are the remains of Honing Station and one of the most fascinating sections of the walk, with something for everyone. A lovely wooded section ends with a truly handsome iron road bridge, well worth a closer inspection. It looks, at first glance, a somewhat flimsy structure, until you see that the horizontal girders are joined by metal ties from which spring brick arches to carry the roadway. It is also one of the few structures along the line where the engineers have allowed themselves a little superfluous decoration to give a touch of grace. Now we are in an area of marsh and fen, reed and sedge, a reminder that we are coming down to the edge of the Broads. Such areas are increasingly rare and so the more welcome.

The final stretch comes as something of a disappointment, a straight run between hedges, though there are more enticing if distant prospects of ploughed fields and church towers. Closer at hand are ample reminders that a town is near – beer cans, sweet wrappers, broken bottles. This is the only place on the line where such delights of an advanced civilization are encountered. So, at last, Stalham is reached, the end of the walk. The good news is that extensions are planned to join the Weavers' Way to the coast. If they offer as many delights as the present route, they will be very welcome.

MANIFOLD TRACK

Route Waterhouses to Hulme End, 8 miles
Map OS 119
Access Waterhouses
Wetton Mill
Swainsley
Hulme End
Cycling Cycle hire, Waterhouses
Leaflet Peak National Park, Derbyshire County Council

If the Weavers' Way seemed only to serve a host of small villages, then the Leek and Manifold Light Railway is even stranger, for it goes from nowhere in particular to nowhere in particular – passing very little else along the way. The 8 miles of the walk represent the full length of the original line, a little railway in every sense, for it was built to a 2-foot 6-inch (76-centimetre) gauge. The Leek and Manifold was born amid the flurry of new lines constructed under the Light Railways Act. Looked at in terms of engineering, it was a great success, built to the very highest standards. In financial terms, it was an utter disaster: opened in 1904, it was closed in 1935. It does, however, have the distinction of being the first of the

Just one of the multitude of bridges that carried the line of the Leek and Manifold Light Railway across the little river Hamps.

old lines to be turned into a public footpath and bridleway when Staffordshire County Council took it over in 1937.

The route begins at the old station at Waterhouses, under the shadow of the great quarries of Caldon Low, which had their own rail and canal connections to Froghall. There is a rather fine canopied goods shed which houses the cycle hire concern, run, as are those of Derbyshire, by the Peak District National Park. This is an ideal starting place for those who are not sure if they can remember how to ride a bike – or are perhaps just uncertain about the state of their leg muscles, for they can enjoy a gentle ride up and down the line on a tarmacked surface. Walkers would probably find this surface rather less to their liking. This was the point where the narrow-gauge line joined the standard gauge to Leek, but the railpath having arrived, at once disappears again at the main road which has to be crossed and followed east for a little way before the path itself is rejoined beside the river Hamps. The river winds and wiggles its way between the enclosing hills, while the railway endeavours to go straight. The result is such a plethora of little bridges that I abandoned the attempt to count them and had to wait until I got back to scrutinize the OS map to come up with the number of twelve river crossings in the first 3 miles. The route goes steadily down hill through a gentle, comfortable landscape of smooth, rounded hills and pleasant woodland – and, one would add beside the pleasant burblings of the river, except that when I came this way there was not a drop of water in it. This is just the sort of countryside you would take a foreign visitor to see if he had expressed the desire to see something typically English. It turned out to be a busy day. A hare bounded along the track in front of me, swerving off into the grass as he met a flock of sheep coming in the opposite direction. The shepherd was extracting the last sheep from a field and I inadvertently became shepherd myself, for they all turned round and went back to where they had started. Fortunately, no-one minded and it proved no more than a pleasant interlude on an attractive day.

After 3 miles, the whole nature of the walk changes quite dramatically as the little Hamps joins the Manifold. Instead of smooth hills, tall limestone crags climb high above the valley floor in a manner very similar to that of Dove Dale to which indeed the Manifold is heading. We, however, are going upstream but towards scenery at least as romantic and picturesque as that of the more famous neighbouring valley. The Manifold Valley is not so narrowly enclosing as Dove Dale, but there is real majesty in its towering peaks, and it has one feature as fascinating as one could wish – Thor's Cave. This vast natural cave can be seen high on the hillside above the track. There was a halt here in the working days of the railway and passengers, when there were any, could get out and climb the steep path to the cave. You can still go there and for those unaffected by vertigo it is well worth the visit, though I cannot promise quite the surprise I had on a previous occasion. My wife and I were walking down from Hulme End when we saw puffs of coloured smoke issuing from the cave mouth while what appeared to be a cloaked and helmeted figure stood at the entrance as though confronting some fearsome dragon. We had to find what was going on – and it was indeed a hero confronting a dragon, but only for the benefit of the cameras on the adjoining hill. We had walked into and interrupted the shooting of a feature film – and the film makers were not in the least pleased to see us, but the hero, who turned out only to be a humble stand-in, did not seem to mind very much.

Back in the valley, the route continues to bend and turn following the line of the river to Wetton Mill, a National Trust property with a small café – but worth a pause, even if you are not in need of refreshment, to admire the stone bridge across the Manifold. For the next mile-and-a-half the route is open to cars:

Opposite Few railways can offer finer scenery than this. The Leek and Manifold once had a halt here for passengers to leave the train to climb up to Thor's Cave high up the hillside. These excursion trains were among the company's few successes.

unfortunately, I should add. They make a noisy intrusion into a very ancient land. There are barrows on Wetton Hill and Thor's Cave was a home for prehistoric man. It means that walkers and cyclists must take special care when going through the 154-yard (140-metre) long Swainsley tunnel, though it is possible to go round it. In fact, the tunnel was not, strictly speaking, needed at all. The company agreed to build it rather than encroach on the grounds of Swainsley Hall.

The tunnel marks another change of mood. The hills no longer fall away in steep crags. Ecton Hill is round and symmetrical, the only scars it bears being not those of natural erosion but those left by the important copper mining industry of the eighteenth century. There is more evidence of early mining as the line crosses the Manifold for the last time and river and railway begin to edge apart. Here, close to the track, is the dark and dripping entrance to a long-abandoned lead mine.

The end of the run is almost a disappointment after the grandeur of the earlier section. A low embankment leads across the fields to a huddle of wooden buildings, which are now a road depot. Once, however, this was the headquarters of the Leek and Manifold Light Railway Company. Here is the old engine house, home for the two locomotives, and the booking office where the company hoped to sell sufficient tickets to fill their four coaches. And if you leave the yard and turn up the road towards the river you will come to the old Railway Hotel. Until recently it gloried in the name 'The Light Railway', and pictures of the line graced the walls but, in 1984, a change of ownership brought a change of name to The Manifold Valley. It is still an excellent friendly place, with real ale and good food, but I cannot help feeling saddened by the change. It was after all another link with the past of this beautiful, if slightly ridiculous, little railway.

This may look like a collection of old sheds, but it was the Hulme End headquarters of the Leek and Manifold. The building on the left was the main administrative and booking office, while that to the right was the original engine shed.

PENCAITLAND WALK

Route	West Saltoun to Crossgatehall, 6½ miles
Map	OS 66
Access	Ormiston Station, B6371
	Pencaitland Station
	Saltoun Station, minor road 1 mile south of West Saltoun
Cycling	
Leaflet	East Lothian District Council

In railway terms, this could be described as the very opposite of the Leek and Manifold for, where the latter appeared to have no function whatsoever, the Pencaitland was very much a line with a role to play in the working world. It is, in fact, not one railway but two: the section leading west from Ormiston was part of the mighty North British empire, while the eastern section was built by the Gifford and Garrald Light Railway, though the small line was soon taken over by the big. Why the rush of railway building in this area? The answer is not immediately apparent but soon becomes so as you begin the walk.

For those tidy minded individuals who like to start logically at one end rather than somewhere in the middle, then the choice is made for you as there is only access to the West Saltoun end of the walk. Although it begins on a minor road south of the village there is no difficulty at all in spotting it, for the old signal post still stands by the roadside with, in place of its signal, a pointer directing you to the line. Across the road is Saltoun Station, a rather grand name for a very small halt. Though the old wooden station buildings remain, any thoughts of trespass are rapidly dispelled by an official notice on the wall warning of terrible cattle diseases lurking within. Here, too, is a battered and steadily decaying passenger

Overleaf Not perhaps the scenery that the average Sassenach thinks of as being typically Scottish, but this rich farmland is certainly very typical of the Pencaitland Walk.

coach serving as farm store. This then is the start, and no hint yet of the purpose for which the line was built.

The scenery perhaps comes as something of a surprise to those who think of Scotland entirely in terms of the dramatic vistas of the Highlands. This is a rich, lush land of gentle hills, with the moorland and the heather no more than a distant prospect. It is a green landscape with every shade of colour from the palest to the darkest, only interrupted by the brilliant yellow patches of the rape fields. First impressions then are of a gentle country that might as easily be in England as Scotland but, when the wind is from the west, a scent is carried along on the breeze that soon removes that illusion. Drifting down the Kinchie Burn comes the aroma from the Glenkinchie distillery where a decidedly fiery lowland malt whisky is produced. Then you arrive at a deep cutting in which the smell is lost and, with its passing, goes the temptation to make an unscheduled detour. The distillery does not, however, constitute the reason for the railway having been built, and another shady, wooded section with a little picnic area does nothing to dispel the feeling that this is an entirely rural line. But beyond this comes the first of what the authorities call history boards but which are in fact carved stones that will now be a regular feature of the route, each one giving details of a colliery that was once worked on this site. Without the board there would be little to tell you that this was the case, yet each board tells a story of men employed, coal dug – and closure. Many of these Lothian pits were opened in the nineteenth century, closed in the pre-war depression years, re-opened in the fuel-hungry, post-war years, and then closed yet again.

If the going now seems easy, this is because you are on a slight slope, at the bottom of which is the village of West Pencaitland, a railway cottage and the indicator still in place to show that you have just descended a 1 in 50 gradient. Here, too, dominating the skyline just as the headstocks of the old collieries had once done, are giant shining metal silos, looking more like borrowings from Cape Canaveral than anything from the world of agriculture. But the feeling of being in a rich agricultural and rural landscape survives the sight of these glistening monsters as the route crosses the main road – the way over still guarded by signal posts even if the signals themselves have long gone. Ahead lies the river Tyne – not the same river as its better-known English namesake. It is crossed on a low bridge which offers pleasant views of the attractive countryside and the somewhat less attractive sewage works alongside. Then the way leads on to Ormiston and the site of the station.

We are at the junction of the two original lines, and also at a point where the nature of the country undergoes a definite change. This is the heart of the old mining district and, if you look up the station in the *Handbook of Railway Stations*, you find no fewer than eleven sidings listed including the very local Ormiston Station Colliery siding. The mine history boards confirm their presence and, soon, physical remains of the collieries also appear. Before that, however, the route enters one of its most open and most attractive sections, running alongside a stream, its banks thick with

The ruins of pithead buildings also mark the line of the Pencaitland Walk and, in spite of its present, essentially rural character, they show the true nature of this former colliery line.

flowers. Then the first signs of the old industry, mentioned so often on the wayside boards, appear in earnest. The natural rise and fall of the ground, such a pleasant feature of the whole walk, is now matched by unnatural undulations, the man-made hills of colliery spoil heaps. Once, when they were part of the working scene, these would have been gaunt, naked intrusions in the landscape. Time has softened them, plants have colonized them, blurring the harsh edges so that one feels that quite soon only the passer-by with the keenest eyesight will recognize these hillocks as intrusions into the natural world. Towards the end of the line, however, this industrial landscape forces itself inescapably to the forefront: the remains of pithead buildings crumble above the line, cascading rubble down the bank. The notice boards appear more frequently here, but are scarcely needed. You can read all you need to know in the ruins and the piles of spoil. In time, no doubt these remains too will collapse back into the landscape to leave little hint of the honeycombs of passages that lie beneath your feet. Nature is already beginning the takeover and, as if to emphasize the point, a hare appeared among the ruins, sniffed the air, and hurried from one side of the track to the other.

We are now very much at the end of the way for, up ahead, industrial life still goes on in the pits and works round Dalkeith. The line is blocked and there is nothing to do but turn away from the industrial present and walk back through the industrial past to the rich green fields. The Pencaitland Walk has provided a fascinating mixture of interests and pleasures, industrial landscape and open country. It is a mixture that one might expect to find in this part of the world, but there may be a few more surprises in store for those setting off on our next walk.

The simple style of railway architecture: the old crossing keeper's cottage still has its sign which informs walkers now, rather than engine drivers, that they are about to leave the flat for a 1 in 50 gradient.

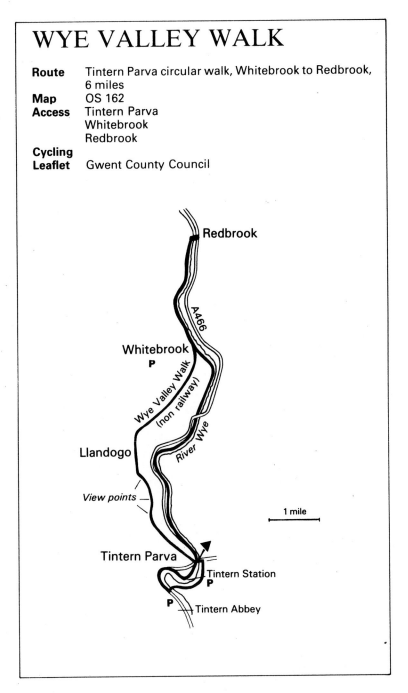

WYE VALLEY WALK

Route	Tintern Parva circular walk, Whitebrook to Redbrook, 6 miles
Map	OS 162
Access	Tintern Parva Whitebrook Redbrook
Cycling	
Leaflet	Gwent County Council

This gentle excursion along the Wye Valley might seem at first to be a complete contrast to the Pencaitland, with its still-obvious connections with industry. Think of the Wye and you probably think of Wordsworth sitting on a hillside admiring the view of Tintern Abbey – though today he would probably have to be content with occasional glimpses of the ruins, spotted in the gaps between tourist coaches. Or perhaps you might think of majestic

Goodrich Castle or the rocks of Symonds Yat rising high over the convolutions of the river. Or, if you know the river more intimately, thoughts might turn to quiet wooded reaches and the pursuit of the salmon. Yet, if you had come here two or three centuries ago, you would probably be making comparisons with Sheffield or some other busy industrial centre. The woods beside the river smoked with the fires of iron furnaces, wire works surrounded the abbey, vessels loaded with copper ore from Cornwall came up the river to unload at the smelters, and the same region sent metal to the tin plate works. By the nineteenth century this great industrial clamour had been partly stilled, but sufficient remained to provide a busy traffic for a railway and, though today you have to search hard to find evidence of that busy industrial past, it is still there, and for me gives the line a special piquancy – a

Sheep graze beneath the signal box at Tintern Parva, perched high above the flood levels of the River Wye. The signal box is just one element in a restored station scene.

line that served God and Mammon with equal efficiency, carrying visitors to the famous abbey and raw material for industry. The line can be enjoyed simply for the pleasures of the scenery, but those with a curiosity about the past will find intriguing traces of that other life of the region.

The Wye Valley Railway was officially opened in 1876, and visitors to Tintern Station at Tintern Parva will have little difficulty in imagining the scene. Thanks to the restoration work of Gwent County Council, the station area looks magnificent. Everything is here except, in spite of a warning to beware of them, the trains. One short length of track has survived on which is a coach, housing a small exhibition showing something of the working life of the line. Here, too, are the station buildings, signal box, ground frame, and signals. There are three short walks laid out from the

Overleaf The iron bridge that once carried the railway across the Wye at Redbrook. The footpath, cantilevered out to the side, is a recent addition.

station, the first and longest of which is the one most likely to interest railway enthusiasts – and possibly even non-enthusiasts as well.

The walk sets off along the track which is carried on an embankment towards Tintern. It does not, however, get very far. At a point where it reaches the river, a gap appears where once a viaduct stood, of which all that remain are the massive abutments. In trying to photograph the site, I was given a sharp reminder of why the embankment was necessary. Balancing on the river bank I found myself starting to slide down towards the water on a greasy slope. The Wye here is tidal and the river rises high: hence my descent and hence the need to build up the railway bank. The walk continues, necessarily, along a non-railway route beside the river to St Michael's Church, where it joins the main road through Tintern, to a girder bridge. Tintern still has some evidence of its industrial past: Quay House stands at the site of the old dock, and by the Royal George are the remains of the last of more than twenty water wheels which once powered forges and iron works. The girder bridge looks like, and is, a railway bridge. It carried a branch of the W.V.R. from the main line on the far bank to the wire works of Tintern. It was hoped that the improvement in transport would bring new life to the decaying industry, but it proved a forlorn hope. The industry had been built on the river and the woods, for water power and charcoal: the world had moved on to other methods and other fuels.

Crossing the bridge, the path turns to the right and you have a fine view of the abbey – not Wordsworth's, he penned his lines from a viewpoint on the opposite bank. A steep path leads up the hillside and then turns off to the left to bring you out above the 182-yard (166-metre) long Tintern tunnel that carried the main line. The path comes down the hill, past a Moravian church, to Brockweir and what appears to be, might have been but is not, a railway bridge. The W.V.R. was given permission to build a bridge to carry tracks across the river at this point, but was very reluctant to go to that expense without some guaranteed traffic to carry. Their experience on the Wireworks Branch persuaded them that the Tintern wireworks was unlikely ever again to show a profit, so they never took their option to build the bridge. The present bridge was built by public subscription in 1906. Returning across the Wye, the line is rejoined at the end of the bridge to provide a pleasing, tree-lined route back to the station.

The railway route forms part of the long-distance Wye Valley Walk, and those who want to continue on foot can follow the path round Llandogo where, among other delights, they will encounter the substantial remains of the seventeenth-century Coed Ithel blast furnace set among the woods. The less energetic can make their way by road through Llandogo, where pub names such as 'The Sloop' (with a fine sign which shows a vessel which is quite definitely not a sloop) offer reminders that this was a busy port until the railway pinched the trade. The railway itself is rejoined at Whitebrook. This is a short section of walk in distance, but those who enjoy the peace of woodland and river may find it long in time, for there is every encouragement to linger. You leave the

The notice commands caution, the signals are set, but the visitor to Tintern Parva Station need not feel too concerned, for trains are most unlikely to pass this way again.

road beside a farm: behind you are the faint traces of the railway leading back towards Tintern, but the track ahead is quite plain. At once you step into the shade of the trees which will stay with you until Redbrook is reached. This is a fine mixture of grand old trees – a wood of oak and birch, sycamore and beech with just an occasional patch of conifer, announced as much by the piney smell in the air as by appearance. Among the trees, flowers bloom and I was there when the bluebells formed a colourful haze over the woodland floor. Birds sing loud and clear, while below you the Wye runs swiftly. There is little to disturb the calm. Occasionally, you catch sight of a fisherman, statue-like in the river, hoping to tempt salmon or trout. He will certainly not disturb you – and would much prefer that you do not disturb him. Years ago my wife and I canoed down this river and, at a point where passage was restricted by rapids flying between the rocks, a fisherman stood. We were descending and he turned in a fury and demanded that we clear off. Quite where we were to clear off to was far from obvious. Once you join the rapids there is no return and little choice of line, a point I would have been prepared to explain had time permitted. As it was we shot past, miraculously missing fisherman and tackle, and paddled on followed by his curses.

There was no-one to curse me as I walked through the woods. Streams tumble and splash down the hillside over mossy boulders while, in places, the tree branches meet over the walker's head to form a green tunnel. Massive rocks can be seen scattered on the hillside, and stone from here was once extensively quarried for use as grindstones, principally for cider presses. Some of these great stones have also been used to form a retaining wall beside the line. The official path diverges from the railway near Redbrook, though the rail track can just as easily be followed. If you take the riverside path, you can still follow the same route, and it does give an opportunity to observe the railway bank and the very substantial stone-arched and stone-lined culverts that carry the hill streams. At Redbrook the line crosses the river on an iron bridge, though the footpath section is a later addition. Beyond this, the railway can easily be followed for a little way through Lord's Grove, but it is also worth pausing at Redbrook itself. This was the site of the last tinplate works in the valley, which only closed in 1961. It is also, to round off the trip with an appropriate railway theme, the site of an early tramway. The Monmouth tramroad ran above the town, and the incline that led down towards the river can be seen and includes a fine bridge across the Newland road. The walk is over: a gentle excursion I said at the beginning, but I doubt if you could find many short walks with such a varied character and such a varied history anywhere else in the country.

An enticing invitation, but there is no point now in waiting on the platform for the race day special. It shows again the care that has gone into bringing the true railway atmosphere back to Tintern.

BATH TO BRISTOL

Route Bath to Staple Hill, 10 miles
Map OS 172
Access Brassmill Lane, Bath
Bitton Station
Cycling

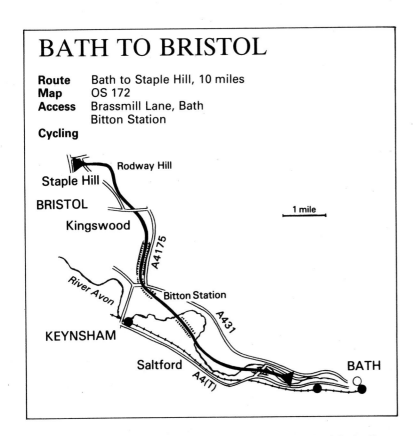

This is not, as you might think, an invitation to walk with the Inter City 125 along the old Great Western route between the two cities. It is not a main line route at all, nor does it form any part of the mighty G.W.R. empire. The line, in fact, does not, strictly speaking, join Bath to Bristol, but Bath to Mangotsfield, where it joined the Gloucester to Bristol line, the whole belonging to the Midland Railway. Looked at in historic terms of the old rivalries between the Great Western and the Midland, one has to say that this is one that went to the G.W.R. The G.W.R. still carries trains, the Midland route is given over to walkers and cyclists. It was opened in 1869 and ran from Bath's Green Park Station, a handsome edifice in its day, built, naturally enough, of Bath stone. The route through the inner city has, however, been lost and can now only be joined at Brassmill Lane, just south of the A4, close to the western edge of the city. Cyclists earn a special mention here for the route was opened up by the volunteer efforts of an excellent organization, Cyclebag, and their Railway Path Project. And a very fine job they have made of it, too.

The first part of the route is very much dominated by the River Avon, which is crossed four times in the first three miles, each time on a girder bridge which, if functional, can scarcely be said to enhance the scene. This is a disappointment to those who travel the Avon by boat, but makes very little difference to those following the railway, who can peer over the parapet at the gentle waters. This is, in fact, a very gentle country route, with the landscape becoming ever more open as you move outwards from Bath. It is a line particularly rich in wild flowers, while the more distant prospects are always enticing, from the wooded slopes below Kelston hill to the reedy river bank and the dark-green fields of barley turning their paler backs to the wind. It shares with the Forest Way we shall be meeting later the distinction of being a delightfully aromatic route. The scent of flowers is heavy on the air and is joined further along the way by more mouth-watering smells. When the wind is in the west the strong, sweet aromas drift across from the chocolate factory at Keynsham and, just beyond that, the pungent smell of cinammon brings thoughts of teacakes and Bath buns.

The line seems scarcely to touch the towns along the way. Saltford appears, dipping its toes into the water's edge, but one

glimpse of houses and water and it is gone. So the towns keep their distance, but distance certainly seems to lend enchantment to the view. Bitton church tower is seen, snuggled down between the hills, and it is complemented close to the line by the swellings of an ancient tumulus. On the other side of the line, Keynsham too keeps its distance, though the bright red brick of the chocolate factory quite dominates the river scene. Keynsham is served by the other rail route, although Bitton has its station on our line, some distance from the village centre, but still intact and, more to the point, still in use. For this is now the home of the Bitton Railway.

The railway society took over an almost derelict station, restored it, and began assembling their collection of what we now think of as the usual mixture of 0–6–0 tank engines and carriages, ready to run a steam line. But they have also gone beyond the

The wheel arrangement might give a hint to the cogniscenti – the 4-6-0 of one of the well-known Stanier Black Five locomotives, awaiting reconstruction at Bitton Station.

norm for steam preservationists. They have goods waggons and a beautifully restored steam crane. There are non-railway exhibits as well: traction engines, steam rollers, and old buses. They are planning a transport museum on the site alongside the steam railway which now runs on nearly a mile of track. There are more ambitious plans for the future. There will be bigger and better locomotives for a start. In the station yard are the dismembered portions of a Black Five which, it is hoped, will soon be back on the tracks and steaming. More ambitious still are the plans for extending the route back to Bath, which will take this little railway out of the short chuff along the line category and into the ranks of those railways which offer a definite trip from one town to another. But how will this affect the walker? If trains are to run again will this mean no more walking and cycling along the line? Not a bit of it, and you can see the solution to that problem already applied in the section beyond Bitton. This was originally a double-track line and, in a sense, still is – for the rails and trains run down one side, while the rest of us, separated off by a wire fence, make our way down the other. The notion of having a steam accompaniment on a walk from Bath to Bristol is one that I find particularly appealing.

At Bitton, the observant will notice traces of an older railway, the tramway built from Keynsham to Mangotsfield by the Kennet and Avon Canal Company to bring coal down to the brass works at Keynsham. The Avon valley was a great centre for brass making, and railways and brass come together at Saltford mill where an unknown hand has carved on a stone the inscription 'Begun Diggin The Rail Road 1836'. Railroad and tramroad remain as close neighbours and, ironically, this brought the Midland right up against the Great Western, for the latter acquired the Kennet and Avon Canal and its tramway.

The line now runs in towards the suburbs of Bristol, but there is no sense of being hemmed in by urbanity – and here, at least, urbanity takes a very pleasing form. And there are occasional breaks in the built-up areas as you come across the commons where the humps and bumps indicate where they were worked for coal. Mangotsfield Junction then arrives, a triangle of routes with the station in the centre, now much worn and ivy clad. The Bristol line heads off to the west and now comes to a halt at the end of a cutting with the boarded-up entrance to Staple Hill tunnel. There are plans to extend the walk further in towards Bristol, but no definite date for when this is likely to be achieved. But it is surely scarcely necessary to point out that, although the line never quite reaches the centre of either of the cities that mark its ends, both are easily accessible and both more than deserve a visit, whether your taste runs to the Georgian elegance of Bath or the Byzantine splendours of the ancient port of Bristol. And what railway enthusiast could really resist Bristol with its memories of Brunel – the Clifton bridge, the SS *Great Britain* and the architectural splendour of the original Temple Meads Station. Even those unimpressed by the delights of the latter will probably end up there anyway – if only to put their feet up and let the train take them back to the starting point in Bath.

Opposite Bitton Station is not only a home for preserved locomotives, it is also home to a fine collection of other steam-powered machinery, including this beautifully restored crane.

STROUD VALLEYS TRAIL

Route   Stonehouse to Nailsworth, 6 miles
Map   OS 162
Access   Stonehouse, car park beside Ship Inn, A419
             Nailsworth, by Railway Hotel A46, car park in town
             centre
Cycling
Leaflet Gloucestershire County Council

Stonehouse

STROUD

A419

Ebley Mill

Woodchester

Woodchester Wool Store

A46

1 mile

Dunkirk Mill

Egypt Mill

NAILSWORTH

The railway has left
Nailsworth – and the
Railway Hotel has certainly
seen better days.

Although this might appear from a glance at the map to be a
typical local branch line, it began life as a fully fledged independent
railway. This was the company's main line: it was, indeed, their
only line. Why should a railway company be formed to build such
a line in the first place, apart from the prevailing Victorian view
that everywhere should have a railway and, to live without one,
was to be reduced to the rank of second-class citizen? The answer
rapidly becomes apparent to anyone visiting the area – wool. This
was the heartland of the West of England woollen trade. Stroud
squats on the map like an octopus, with the radiating river valleys
as its tentacles, and along these rivers the mills were built. Looking
at my OS map for the region, I see that I have marked off no fewer
than eighteen mill sites on this 6-mile stretch, three of which are
among the biggest and most impressive of the entire region.

Unlike the hotel, Nailsworth station is enjoying a revival in its fortunes: grass may be growing over the old track bed but the station buildings have been converted into a family home.

Unhappily for the Stonehouse and Nailsworth Railway Company, the start of work on their line proved to be a masterpiece of ill-timing. Work was begun in February 1867 just at the time when the local wool trade was about to enter a period of disastrous decline, with the work force halving in the 1870s. The little line also succumbed, being swallowed up by the Midland, and that turned out not to be altogether a good thing. A short spur from Dudbridge was intended to link up with the main line from Stroud, but that was G.W.R. territory, and the two companies were not much given to co-operation. Each went its independent way. There was a thriving coal trade from the Severn via the Stroudwater Canal to Nailsworth – and we shall meet evidence of that trade when we arrive at Nailsworth. In the early days, there was also a passenger service, though that ended in 1947, and then in 1966 freight travel also ceased. The line was closed.

The route starts in the Frome valley to the west of Stroud beside the Ship Inn – a name which, this far inland, almost certainly indicates the presence of a canal, and so it proves to be: the Stroudwater, which joins the Thames and Severn to link those two rivers. It is often said that railways killed off the canals, but here the opposite might be said to be the case for, when canal traffic ceased in the 1920s, the railway trade plummeted. Now, both the old routes are seeing a revival: the railway as a footpath, while the

Stroudwater and Thames and Severn Society have begun the long process of bringing the canals back to life.

Canal and railway meet almost immediately, the latter crossing the former on a very elegant iron bridge, though you need to get down on the towpath to appreciate it. The railway now keeps the canal company for a couple of miles and, across the fields, you might well see the restorers at work with their dredgers. Soon, however, the bordering trees close in on the railway, shutting off the noise of traffic from the nearby main road, but not closing off the view of the splendid scenery. We are just on the edge of the Cotswold escarpment, and the hills rear up ahead and on either side, climbing out of the Severn plain. It is not, perhaps, a very dramatic landscape but it is rich and varied, the hills rounded and lush. It is also an area to gladden the heart of the industrial archaeologist for, very soon, the first of the woollen mills appears in view. This is Stanley Mill to the south of the line and something of an architectural anachronism for, in a county where the beautiful Cotswold stone proliferates, this is mostly red brick. It might sound a little dull but anyone who has ever been inside would never think of such a description – splendid, beautiful, glorious, these are the terms that come to mind. Built in 1813, it was constructed on the basis of brick arches springing from iron columns. The interior consists of colonnades joined by delicate tracery and everywhere the detailing is quite superb.

Those with little or no interest in industrial architecture need not worry for there is plenty more to enjoy here. Farms and houses, built of the rich local stone, sit comfortably in the folds of the hills – though it perhaps should be added that the prosperity that they evince was built upon the mills anyway. The little river appears at regular intervals, its banks lined with almost equal regularity by willows and anglers. It is hard to think of this area as ever having been one of the great industrial centres of the country, for today it seems to epitomize rural peace: a cow saunters nonchalantly down the line, a grass snake sways across it and, even when industry does appear, it is not instantly recognizable. Ebley Mill could well pass as a grand hotel in the continental manner, its chateau-style roof lending an air of French elegance to the building. Mill chimney and weir give the game away but the group remains just as attractive a feature in the landscape as if it had indeed been built for leisure rather than commerce.

Beyond Ebley, the route suddenly comes to an abrupt halt. This is Dudbridge, where the spur so long remained as an unusable route unable to make the connection to Stroud and earning the line the local name 'The Dudbridge Donkey'. It proves equally irritating to present-day walkers who find themselves confronted by a filled-in road bridge totally blocking the way. The cyclists following the route are faced by a considerable detour round the back streets but walkers need only hop over a wall to rejoin the track. There are plans to clear the bridge hole, but someone has to find the money to do it. Here are the remains of a station and the spur to Stroud, but the main route swings away southwards towards Nailsworth, following a route along a shelf cut into the side of the hill.

Opposite Ebley Mill seen from the railway embankment. This is an unusually handsome woollen mill, given a strangely foreign air by its chateau-style roof and tower.

Another woollen mill –
Dunkirk Mill is, in fact, a
major mill complex begun
in the eighteenth century
and regularly extended by
new building over more
than a hundred years.

   This stretch provides an opportunity to compare the industrial
past with the industrial present and, for this observer at least, the
past has no competition. I am not talking about efficiency,
productivity, and the like, but on the place of industry in the
landscape. The old mills, built of local stone, are scarcely
distinguishable from the larger country houses, so comfortably do
they sit within their surroundings. The new factories, the engineering
works which have taken over from the old woollen mills, are
without exception faceless, anonymous piles. Built of synthetic
materials in a dreary unimaginative style, they give the impression
that no-one ever cared a damn about their visual effect – and quite
probably no-one did. Previous generations no doubt used local
designs and local materials simply because they were immediately
available, but the result is a series of buildings which blend into the
landscape and improve and mature with the years. The best that
can be hoped for the recent building is that, when their days of

usefulness are ended, they will rapidly collapse. But, to set against that in the Britain of the 1980s, is the fact that they are being used for production – sadly, an increasingly rare phenomenon.

The walk past the new industries of Stroud could scarcely be called attractive, but it is a short stretch of line and the screen of trees maintains a good deal of the essentially rural character of the route. When I walked the line, the surfaced section ended temporarily by the Woodchester road bridge – which seemed a good excuse to explore this attractive village and visit a local watering hole. The route does, in fact, continue as a path that joins the main road which is then followed for a few hundred metres before the railway walk re-appears as a surfaced path in an avenue of trees. For the remainder of the journey, the pathway will appear and disappear, but walkers who keep an eye open for a likely line, and remember the adage that railways keep on the level, will have few problems. For a while, the way is tarmacked, then again becomes a rough footpath taking a route well up the hillside above the mills and factories that jostle in the valley floor. Here, however, you will find many of the mellow old buildings where the history of their past can be read in their stones. The line runs above Dunkirk Mill, begun in the eighteenth century and extended through the nineteenth, each generation adding its own section in a slightly different style, yet preserving the essential unities. And, anticipating slightly, at the end of the route is Egypt Mill which received its curious name from one of its early owners Mr Pharaoh Webb. It is a stone-built mill with two water wheels fitting into the tight space between road and river. Its appeal lies in its sense of belonging, from its foundations to its stone slate roof.

The end arrives at Nailsworth where the station has now been converted into a private home and the lines ran down into the station yard. Here a warehouse still announces in fading letters that coal is available by the truck load at colliery prices. Even more faded, the Station Hotel has abandoned its wait for passengers who will now never arrive. The railway may be dead, but Nailsworth thrives, a delightful town to explore at the end of an equally delightful walk.

The railway has gone, reduced to a walkway, but the waterway being crossed by the bridge is being restored to use by the Stroudwater and the Thames & Severn Canal Society.

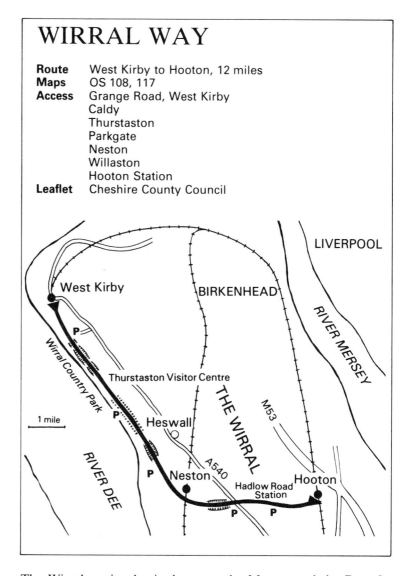

WIRRAL WAY

Route West Kirby to Hooton, 12 miles
Maps OS 108, 117
Access Grange Road, West Kirby
Caldy
Thurstaston
Parkgate
Neston
Willaston
Hooton Station
Leaflet Cheshire County Council

LIVERPOOL

West Kirby

BIRKENHEAD

RIVER MERSEY

Wirral Country Park

Thurstaston Visitor Centre

THE WIRRAL

M53

1 mile

Heswall

RIVER DEE

Neston

A540

Hadlow Road Station

Hooton

Opposite There are times when it seems that the Wirral Way will be almost overwhelmed by nature. Wild roses hang above the track near Heswall.

The Wirral peninsula sits between the Mersey and the Dee. Its eastern flank is dominated by Birkenhead and looks across to Liverpool and the industrial world of Lancashire. Its western side is very different, facing across the Dee to the hills of Wales. On the Wirral, if you make enough money on one side, you can afford to live on the other. The railway served the rich commuter colony and, as the rich commuters began to change from trains to cars, so the bowler hats thinned on the station platforms and the line headed towards inevitable closure. The two ends of the walk are still connected, if somewhat tortuously, via the remaining line up the east of the Wirral, so that it is possible to do a round trip by foot and train.

The start of the walk can be found across the road from West Kirby station. One feature of the way, which could well be copied by others, is the separation of footpath and bridleway. Bridleways

can so easily be churned into quagmires, that one is very grateful for one's own self-contained path – though cyclists are understandably aggrieved at being cut off from the path altogether. The first part of the line passes through the town but, as much of the way is in a leafy cutting, there is no great sense of this being an urban route. In any case, this lasts for no more than a mile before the line emerges into the open and begins to head off towards the coast. There are glimpses of wide expanses of mud and sand, through which the Dee has carved a web of channels as it squirms off down to the sea. Once, this was a major shipping route and Chester an important port but, over the years, navigation has been steadily reduced so that now just a few yachts and dinghies remain. Much of the line being enclosed by trees, you get no more than glimpses of the estuary and the distant hills.

West Kirby behind you, Caldy appears, once a fishing village but now a suburb that stretches down the coast. If the sample census I conducted during my walk is accurate, then the canine population of Caldy outnumbers the human by at least two to one. Everywhere dogs were being walked, which means that human

Only one platform remains of the old Thurstaston Station, and the gate below the bridge proclaims that the former Birkenhead Joint Railway is now a footpath.

walkers must take care about where they place their feet. The village climbs up the hill from the shore and, higher up the hill, the grander houses look down from lofty eminences. Beyond this, the way becomes more open as the line hugs the coast, not by engineers' choice but at the dictates of the wealthy. Thomas Ismay, the famous head of the White Star shipping line had his home at Dawpool Hall, Thurstaston. The railway was anxious to scoop up as many commuters as possible but Ismay wanted it kept at arms' length – and Ismay won. The line passes a mile away from the village, which was the villagers' loss but the walkers' gain for, although much of the line is in a shallow cutting, it is never far from the estuary. At Thurstaston Station, now reduced to a single platform, is the Visitors' Centre, beyond which the route is carried on a slight embankment. Here, the nature of the estuary begins to change. Instead of mud flats and sand, the estuary here becomes clogged with vegetation through which the water makes its sluggish way. Then, civilization begins to close in again with the approach to Heswall.

Unfortunately, before anyone got round to the notion that the old line could be used as a linear country park, sections were sold off for property development. Temporarily, the rough path is deserted for paved streets. You walk down Davenport Road, which meets Station Road, but not alas any station, and then on down Riverbank Road. Here at the edge of the built-up area, the route is rejoined as it heads off towards Gayton, a village whose identity seems largely to have been lost in its engorgement by its larger neighbour. Now we are nearly at the end of the estuary walk and also at its most interesting section. The marshland is rich in

Looking out from the railway at Thurstaston across the Dee estuary.

bird life and is, indeed, a bird sanctuary, while Parkgate when it appears puts on a very maritime appearance. Just before the line drops into a deep cutting, you catch a glimpse of a row of houses facing the water looking, with their boarding and wide expanses of glass, like the bridges of ocean liners. As a friend lives in one of them, I can report that the interiors are even more liner-like, with veneer panels that could have graced the state room of a Cunard Queen – perhaps the proximity of the great Ismay had its effect.

As at Heswall, development has obscured part of the route, and again you must take to the side roads, to another Station Road and Mellock Lane. But when the line does reappear it does so in majestic fashion. There is also a change in style. The line so far was built in the 1880s, but this is an earlier portion dating from the 1860s, and bridges are now in stone rather than brick. Stone there was in plenty, for the cutting on the line went through solid rock, the richly coloured sandstone that is such a feature of the Wirral. It is a real joy on a hot, humid afternoon to pass into the cool cutting with its spreading canopy of trees. It is a double pleasure for there is a decidedly steep gradient at this point, which has been known to cause a deal of trouble to panting engines as well as gasping walkers. The line now is turning away from the sea but not away from the wealth of the Wirral. It is leafy, green, and rich with flowers that almost threaten to engulf the line. Beyond this bright, speckled wilderness all is neatness and order, ruled lines of flower beds beside immaculate lawns. The houses are large and one at least was preparing for its social event of the year, for a marquee the size of a circus tent covered the lawn. But this view of rich living is no more than an interruption to this stroll down a line that now has all the character of a leafy country lane. There is a brief, but not very welcome, eruption of noise as the route passes under the dual carriageway of the A540; then it is on to Willaston and the one surviving station on the line.

Hadlow Road Station was once a busy little spot with more than fifty stopping trains a day, though it is hard to imagine where the passengers might have come from. It has been beautifully restored not, for a change, in the style of one of the old companies who ran the line, but in the colours of those who had charge when the last train ran, British Rail. Track has been laid, level crossing gates are in place, and the home signal quite correctly set at 'stop'. Milk churns and trunks await collection on the platform; the booking office is hung with the fading photographs of old railwaymen; the signal box stands ready for action. It is a splendid piece of work, and it would certainly come as no surprise if the distant sound of a steam whistle were to be heard from around the bend.

After that, anything would seem an anticlimax, but then this is not really a line for big, dramatic gestures. Its pleasures are those of the quiet estuary and the peaceful countryside, and the latter remains right up to the end and the final curve round into Hooton Station. That turns out to be a building as full of character as its restored neighbour down the way. As I stopped to enquire about the trains back to West Kirby I chatted to the toothless porter. For him, at least, the Wirral Way had a reality in vivid memories to match that which the rest of us can only supply from imagination.

WORTH WAY AND FOREST WAY

Route   Groombridge to Three Bridges, 17 miles
Maps   OS 187, 188
Access   Three Bridges Station
             Grange Road, Crawley Down
             East Grinstead Station
             Forest Row, car park behind Foresters' Arms
             Groombridge, railway station
Cycling
Leaflets East Sussex and West Sussex County Councils

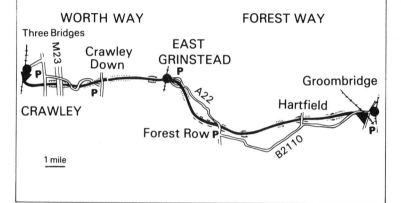

The two names reflect both the fact that a county boundary falls across the line and also that this, although a continuous rail route, was developed in two parts. The first part of the line from East Grinstead to Three Bridges was first authorized in 1846 when the initial plans were laid by John Urpeth Raistrick, a distinguished name in railway history. Raistrick spans the tramway and railway ages, for he was the builder of the Stratford-Moreton tramway and then went on to such important lines as the Grand Junction Railway and the London to Brighton. This line was completed in 1855 and, eleven years later, the London, Brighton, and South Coast Railway built the extension to Groombridge. The two lines were united as a single branch and, walking the routes, there is little to distinguish the one from the other: if anything, judging from the scale of engineering, one would be tempted to reverse the chronology for it is the older route which has the more dramatic works. How the individual tackles the line depends very much on where you start. Energetic Londoners can catch a train to one end, march resolutely to the other and then catch a train home. For a more leisurely approach, you can take it in two stages.

Driving down from Oxfordshire, I worried about the state of the weather, for here was Henley Regatta in progress – and a beautiful, steam launch excited my envy on the way through the town – and Wimbledon was in its first week. Surely it must rain. But no – it was one of those glorious, golden June days that can make England seem for a while the most desirable place in the world. As I set off on the walk, the jets from Gatwick were thundering off towards the Mediterranean, and welcome: they had nothing to offer to match the prospects that lay before me.

Like many deserted lines the Forest Way has been largely lost in its path through the town. But, you can begin in East Grinstead at the official starting place on Herontye Drive off the A22. The route leads south-east from here, but it is worth looking to the north as well where a minor footpath is crossed by a remarkably ornate stone bridge. You might wonder what a housing estate on the edge of East Grinstead has done to deserve such splendour but, in fact, this was once parkland and the nineteenth-century gentleman was liable to demand a little extra decoration as part of the price paid for allowing the railway to invade his land. The walk proper, to the south, at once earns its title of 'Forest Way', for it is a very woody beginning, the route closed off by oak, beech, and birch that join branches overhead to form a cool, green tunnel. The air is pervaded with the scent of flowers and the rich, deep aroma of woodland and leaves; then as the trees thin to give glimpses of pasture, there is the equally sweet, strong smell of hot cattle under a high sun. All blend to produce a scent as English as the wild rose. It is hard not to break into poetic outbursts for this particular walk offers what seems to me to be a perfect example of a particular kind of English landscape, a land of river and meadow, copse and spreading woodland. It is a land with no particular dominant features, nothing to stop you in your tracks with amazement but, rather, a landscape that steadily and rhythmically accumulates small pleasures. It might be the gentle

This ornate stone bridge carries the Forest Way across a housing estate on the edge of East Grinstead, but what is now a modern estate was once a gentleman's park – hence the grandeur.

Overleaf This gentle stream cutting through the meadows beside the Forest Way will swell and grow on its journey eastwards to the sea, for these are the upper reaches of the River Medway.

movement of a field of grain stirred in the light breeze or horses clustered in the deep shade of a giant horse chestnut. And the few houses seem to belong to this world, their walls hung with rich, red tiles. If ever there was an idyllic landscape which an Englishman might dream of away from home, then this is it. There may be some who regard this as almost too perfect, too gentle a country – and, as a northerner, I find it fails to produce that special stirring of the blood which comes with the sight of the sharp, rocky spine of the Pennines – but, in its own terms on a perfect summer's day, it has its magic. And do not be fooled by present-day appearances. The air may now be full of the song of birds and the hum of bees, but once these woods rang with a harsher sound, of hammer on metal. Local names, such as Furnace Wood and Hammer Wood, help to remind us that, as late as the eighteenth century, this was the heart of the iron-making industry of Britain. This is the Weald of which Kipling wrote:

Out of the Weald, the secret Weald,
Man cast in ancient years
The horse-shoes red at Flodden Field,
The arrows at Poitiers!

There are also occasional signs of other activities, guaranteed to remind you of a rapidly growing thirst on a hot day: the oast houses where hops were sent for roasting before ending up in a pint of ale.

Oast houses, more than any other buildings, seem to typify south-east England. Their attractive shapes gladden the walker's eye and encourage a pause for admiration, though association of ideas might send him hurrying on towards opening time.

And what of the railway in all this? To be honest, it scarcely seems to register. Of all the old railways I have walked, this is the one which seems to have best contrived to turn itself into a fair imitation of a quiet, country lane. Only the occasional bridges and the stations at Hartfield and Betts Green, converted into houses, bring any railway thoughts at all. There is, however, one point where the track crosses the main road at Forest Row that you have to think seriously about railways. The bridge has gone, so you need to keep your eye on the likeliest line of the tracks, and that brings you to a surfaced path which runs past the waterworks and the old station yard to rejoin the easily distinguished route that leads on to the main line at Groombridge.

The other section of line, the Worth Way, has a determinably railway beginning in the East Grinstead station car park. There would be a good case for changing names here, for this is a forest way in every sense, scarcely ever emerging from the cover of trees. It starts by sneaking out of town unnoticed, disappearing into a deep, dark cutting which can be made even darker by a cover of leaden clouds. Having survived the combination of Henley and Wimbledon on the previous day, the addition of the first day of the Test Match proved too much. The tree-shaded route did, however, provide a useful shelter from the spats of rain that appeared every now and then. The map tells you of many interesting sites just off the line, such as the sixteenth-century timber-framed manor house of Gullege Farm, but they tend to be hidden behind the ever-present screen of trees. What can be seen is water, ponds both near at hand and glistening in the distance. These were formed to provide a good head of water for the wheels that powered the big hammers of the woodland forges, though today they are only valued for their decorative place in the landscape and the fish in their waters.

The Worth Way has an unfortunate habit of performing disappearing acts. At Crawley Down it reaches the edge of a big estate where, theoretically, it remains signposted – but where most of the signs have been vandalized. To thread your way through this maze, go down Cob Close and straight along Hazel Way to the end, where you are faced with a footpath which you follow to Copse Close. Here you turn left, cross the road and find, with a feeling of some relief at being back on familiar territory, Old Station Close which takes you back to the line. I shall not bore the reader with an account of all the wrong turnings I made before sorting out that route.

The cutting on the edge of town is far and away the deepest on the line, a strangely secluded world after the new streets and houses at Crawley Down. Then, just as you are beginning to feel back at home again, another diversion appears – though a much more pleasant one. The ground of the old Rowfant Station has been taken over by industry. The line is carried on an embankment, but the path drops away through woodland at the side of the route and rejoins it beyond the last of the station buildings.

One last tree-lined section takes the line to a minor road just short of the M23 and, yet again, the railway is lost. The Worth Way turns south along the road before joining a quiet footpath

The Forest Way today has few reminders of its railway past, and this peaceful crossing could easily be any gateway leading out from any country lane – little to show that it is a railway crossing.

that goes on for just over a mile before rejoining the original route for the last few hundred metres to Three Bridges. It is undeniably a pleasant walk through some lovely wooded country but it is also very frustrating to be constantly diverted from one's chosen track. For those who like a sense of completeness in their endeavours, then the combination of Forest Way and Worth Way does give you the whole line but, for those who might in any case find 17 miles a little daunting, I would recommend the Forest Way as the more satisfactory of the two. It is an almost perfect piece of rural England and makes quite a contrast to our next two routes, though perhaps not quite so strong a contrast as you might expect.

NEWPORT PAGNELL BRANCH

Route   Newport Pagnell to Wolverton, 4 miles
Map   OS 152
Access   Broad Street, Newport Pagnell
Cycling

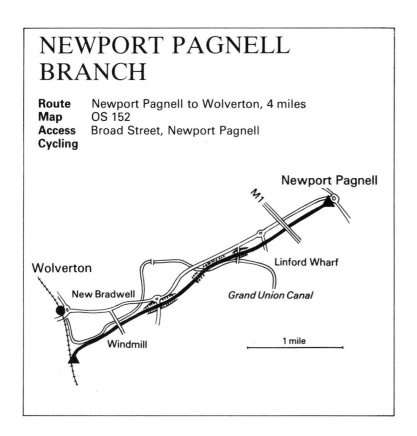

A feature of recent years has been the growth of new towns to relieve the pressures on London – and the appearance of one new city, Milton Keynes. At this stage in its development, it is often quite difficult to decide when you are in Milton Keynes at all, the only hint being the proliferation of roundabouts in the middle of nowhere and signposts pointing you to mysterious destinations known only as MK 14 and the like. Among the new development are the old towns and villages, including Newport Pagnell and, among the new transport routes, are the old. There is the coaching road that once passed this way, the Grand Union Canal and, of course, the railway. This walk gives a fascinating insight into the importance of transport routes in shaping the landscape, and also shows what a local authority can do to make the most out of the old routes.

Newport Pagnell has little importance in railway history, as its branch line was never any more than a short spur off the main line, serving to bring the delights of rail travel to the good citizens of the town. When we look at Wolverton at the other end of the line, however, we find something quite different. Here we have a town built by the railway and for the railway, as important in its day as Crewe or Swindon. The London and Birmingham Railway was one of the first major trunk routes of Britain and, as with other early railways such as the Great Western, it needed works for the manufacture and repair of locomotives and rolling stock – preferably set somewhere near the centre of the line. Wolverton is

The railway estate of New Bradwell was built to house workers at the nearby Wolverton works. Little now remains, but this street at least has been refurbished in splendid style.

not quite in the middle, but it is near enough and was very conveniently situated by the canal, along which building materials could be brought. It never quite achieved the prominence which its planners had anticipated for, when the London and Birmingham was absorbed into the London and North Western Railway in 1846, locomotive building was concentrated at Crewe and Wolverton was left with just its carriage works. It remained, and remains, an important place in the railway world – and it is to Wolverton that our walk will take us.

The walk begins just by the site of the old Newport Pagnell Station, now demolished. The authorities have really taken this old route to their hearts, giving it the four-star treatment – tarmac throughout its length, lighting along the way, signposts and a few preserved features to remind users that this was indeed once a busy little line. The Milton Keynes planners seem to have been aware that a recurring problem in new towns is their anonymity, that sense of being dropped on to the landscape with little concern for what was there before. They have done their best to highlight those features they inherited, including walks that have been set out both here on the railway and on the nearby canal towpath. It soon becomes clear during the walk that they were wise to take such measures.

It all begins pleasantly enough as the route takes you along behind some well-kept allotments, but then the view disappears behind a screen of trees that is an almost continual accompaniment for the rest of the way. Through the gaps, however, you can see the steady march of housing as the Milton Keynes expansion gets into its stride. This is not yet an urban walkway – but it soon will be. The value of a pedestrian and cycle route will grow as the town grows and road traffic increases. Very soon, too, it becomes clear just why the whole place was put here for, if we are walking towards a railway town, then we are certainly walking through a motorway city. The wide bridge of the M1 spans the line with that constant procession of cars and trucks that did as much as anything to turn this little railway into a walkway.

It comes as something of a surprise after walking many disused lines, suddenly to come upon a reminder that there are still working railways in Britain: a busy main line scene at Wolverton.

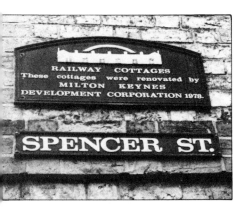

Spencer Street in New Bradwell has not just been restored; the authorities have placed this plaque on the wall to make sure its historic importance is appreciated.

Opposite A rusting loco-motive lurks among the rubble of a scrapyard above the cutting that once carried the Newport Pagnell branch line through New Bradwell.

Beyond the motorway there are glimpses of extensive sand and gravel pits and then the canal which has been running alongside, but out of sight, is crossed on a girder bridge. Pausing by the bridge, I contemplated the fate of these two routes. The old Grand Junction Canal, now the Grand Union, was modernized and improved but ultimately fell to the same road transport competition that killed its other rival, the railway. Now both have found a new use as routes for leisure not trade. The old line I was walking was busy with bicycling families while pleasure boats were moored along the canal. At least they are both still in use, and both well used at that.

No-one could describe this as an especially scenic route. There are occasional glimpses of new housing estates and even a sight of the countryside, but always the trees close in again. Then you reach a station platform, an old halt which a sign announces as New Bradwell. Those who know their railway history will now feel a sudden quickening of interest, and they will not be disappointed. I left the cutting and climbed the ramp up to the road bridge. New Bradwell was a railway suburb, built by the company for its employees at the nearby Wolverton works, a reminder that up until 1876 the railway had been the sole large employer in the town. I was expecting something of interest, but not what I actually found. I reached the road and there next to the bridge was a scrapyard. Among the wrecked cars and discarded gas cookers stood, sad but dignified, an old saddle tank locomotive, still complete but rusted and decaying. I paused to pay my respects then walked across the canal and on into the town. Originally, there was a grid of streets lined with railway cottages, but most have now gone. One street, Spencer Street, still remains, superbly renovated by Milton Keynes Development Corporation and run as a housing co-operative. The buildings form simple, two-storey terraces with three-storeyed houses set at the ends – and very handsome and attractive they look. They can stand comparison with the better-known renovation of the railway houses of Swindon. Milton Keynes has received a lot of criticism over the years, but full marks here for a job well done.

Back on the line, there was one piece of renovation to admire. A fine tower windmill stands just above the track. There is something satisfying about the contemplation of power in this sense. From this survivor of wind power, you look down on the route of steam power and beyond to the canal which, for many years, depended on horse power. Then, as you continue the walk for another half mile, you reach electric power – the present London to Birmingham main line.

This is the end of the railway walk proper, for it was here that the branch itself ended, but the walkway continues and it is worth following it a little further. It swings round in a wide curve to a bridge that crosses the main line and the multiple tracks of the railway works. This is Wolverton, still busy, still a railway town. You can continue to the town centre or just stand and watch the busy movement of trains at the point where railway past and railway present meet.

PARKLAND WALK

Route   Finsbury Park to Alexandra Palace, 4 miles
Map   *London A–Z*
Access   Oxford Road, Finsbury Park, N4
             Muswell Hill Road, N10, next to the primary school
             Alexandra Palace Grounds
Leaflet Haringey Parks Services

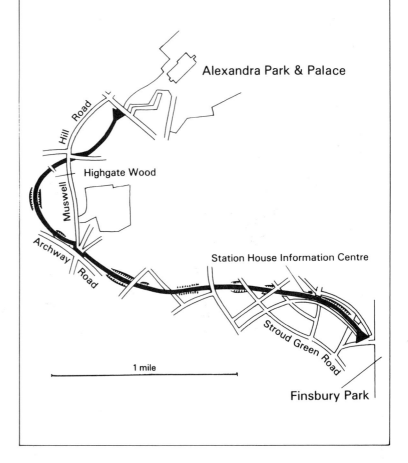

This is very much a country walk through the town, a green leafy way through the heart of London. It also has a special quality which is particularly appealing. Some years ago I wrote an account of a trip round England by canal which I called *Back Door Britain*, because canals generally slide around the backs of houses rather than pass respectably by the front door. The same is true of railways, and this is very much Back Door London. Indeed, the faint sense of voyeurism which you might feel on boating past the end of someone's garden is even stronger here as you stride high above it, looking down on the sleeping baby, the rhubarb patch, and the endlessly fishing gnome.

Just another London road
and another railway bridge
– but this particular bridge
across Stapleton Road
carries the Parkland Walk;
and Station House, next to
the bridge, houses the local
information centre.

The line began life in 1867 as part of the Edgware, Highgate
and London Railway, a company which soon succumbed to its
more influential neighbours. It was absorbed into the Great
Northern Railway which, in the 1920s regrouping, was itself
absorbed into the London and North Eastern Railway. The branch
to Alexandra Palace was started a little later in 1873, but managed
to maintain its independent link with the Palace grounds right up
to 1911. Closure was inevitable, once plans to absorb the line into
the London Transport system were abandoned. With tubes and
buses offering regular, cheap passenger services and no freight to
carry, closure arrived in 1954 when the last passenger train ran.
This was not quite the end of the story for the line was used for a
time to transfer tube trains from Drayton Park. But, in 1970, that
too came to an end and, after a century of use, the working life of
the railway expired. The present walk incorporates the major part
of this line.

Starting at the Finsbury Park end, the first thing that becomes
clear is that it is wise to leave the car at home, for parking spaces
are not so much scarce as non-existent. But a short walk from the
tube down Oxford Road brings you to the railway embankment
which, when I visited, was just in the process of being landscaped.
A short climb up rough steps brings you to the roof-top-level line,
but not a continuous panoramic view, for trees have vigorously
colonized the route – oak, willow, the ubiquitous sycamore and a
good deal of silver birch. They all help to give an amazingly

countrified feel to this city route, an effect much enhanced by the trees and shrubs in the gardens that reach out to the foot of the embankment. So peaceful and rural does it seem that it comes as quite a shock to reach the first bridge and peer down on to the rows of Victorian terraces and the busy traffic of the streets. The effect of two separate and quite different worlds co-existing but somehow never quite making contact is reinforced if you pass from one to the other. Stop off at Station House on Stapleton Road, now an information centre; stand down on the pavement, and look up the line – it is just another of those brick bridges that appear so often across London streets – no hint of the rural walkway you have so recently left.

This almost total divorce between the world of the railway and the world of the streets is again accentuated as cutting follows embankment. Even if you have lived in North London for many years (my first London flat in Avenue Road was only metres from the line) it is virtually impossible to estimate just where you are in relation to the streets. Not that it matters a great deal, because the walk proves to be a delightful stroll, especially in the sun, and there is company in plenty along the way. Families amble, and when I was there, an artist had set up his easel to paint one of the brick bridges and, rather more surprisingly, a young man had brought chair and music stand to the line and was assiduously practising the tenor saxophone, no doubt to the relief of the neighbours if not to the delight of the walkers. And children – there are children everywhere along the way, and very well provided for they are, too. Play areas have been set out and a children's club, gaudily bright in the sun, stands above the cutting. I was, however, delighted to find that for two small boys at any rate, their greatest entertainment seemed to be obtained from playing trains between the derelict platforms, all that remain of the old Crouch End Station. It was local children, too, who kindly invited me to view their secret discovery. In the branches of a sapling beneath the arch of a bridge was a blackbird's nest with three pale-blue eggs in it. They had pulled branches and leaves around this to keep it safe from vandals and were keeping an eager watch for the first signs of hatching.

Shepherd's Hill rises in the path of the line, which ends abruptly at a fine double-arched bridge, now blocked in. The walker has two options. The suggestion made by the official leaflet is that you continue to keep your walk as rural as possible by turning down Shepherd's Hill and taking the track beside the library to Priory Gardens. There you turn right and carry on for a short way until a path is reached that leads to Queen's Wood, which is crossed to Highgate Wood where the railway walk is rejoined. This is certainly a very pleasant way to follow, for the mature woodland is one of London's most attractive green areas, busy with the activities of pigeons and squirrels. Those determined to follow the railway at all costs must go to the top of Shepherd's Hill and follow fume-ridden Archway Road as far as Muswell Hill and Highgate Woods. The railway follows a route between the road and the southern edge of the woods, but is inaccessible for some way as it runs beside the still-busy Northern Line. Only when it swings away

north does it become safe to allow the public near it, and it reappears as a line still clinging to the edge of the wood, but now so overgrown that railway and wood are all but indistinguishable.

There is a brief interruption again at Muswell Hill Road, where a school has been built over the track bed but, after that, Parkway Walk and railway walk again coincide for the route through Muswell Hill. The place and the railway have, in the past, enjoyed a very intimate relationship. The whole area was built up in the 1900s, constructed almost entirely of red brick, and it was along this railway that the bricks were carried. Muswell Hill no longer needs its railway for transport but has at least acknowledged its debt by its treatment of the old line. This is one of the most delightful sections of the route. When I came in the spring, the banks blazed with yellow broom beneath a blue sky. In summer, as I remember well from the days when I lived close by, it is also a splendid spot for blackberrying. You could hardly find a more cheerful scene, which at least prevents one's thoughts from dwelling too long on the horrific tragedy of mass murder executed just a few metres away in Cranley Gardens.

The one thing you probably do not expect to find on such a route is railway engineering on any grand scale, yet here it comes,

The disused urban railway provides a splendid – and safe – playground for the kids. They certainly make full use of the line here in the heart of north London, where the sides of a cutting make an ideal obstacle course for bicycles.

The end of the line for the
Parkland Walk arrives with
the splendour of Alexandra
Palace, still impressive even
after the disastrous fire of
1980.

almost at the end of the line – the long viaduct that stretches across
St James's Lane and carries the route high above the Edwardian
villas. From up here there is a panoramic view over London but, in
the foreground, there is a closer view of the Royal Oak – perhaps
time to pause for a pint and ploughman's. The route ends in the
underpass of Muswell Hill at the primary school where my own
children started their education. But, if you walk into the park,
you can still see the line running up to the station at Alexandra
Palace itself. 'The People's Palace', they used to call it, planned to
be the Crystal Palace of North London. It somehow never quite
made it, and workmen are still coping with the results of a
disastrous fire in 1980. No-one could ever describe the Alexandra
Palace as a huge success. It always looked cumbersome in contrast
with the light airiness of the Crystal Palace but at least it has a
splendid situation, offering spectacular views over the city. The
dome of St Paul's stands out, not quite obliterated by the new
towers of London – and, on a clear day, you can see the aerial that
marks the site of the other palace to the south. There are plenty of
people who look on the old place with affection and hope to see it
in use again one day – rather like the railway really. For that too
still inspires affection and, in its new form, it is very much back in
business.

POTTERIES GREENWAY

Route   Kidsgrove to Hanley, 7 miles
Map   OS 118
Access Numerous access points along the route or via Park
        Farm Golf Course (*see* text for details)
Cycling

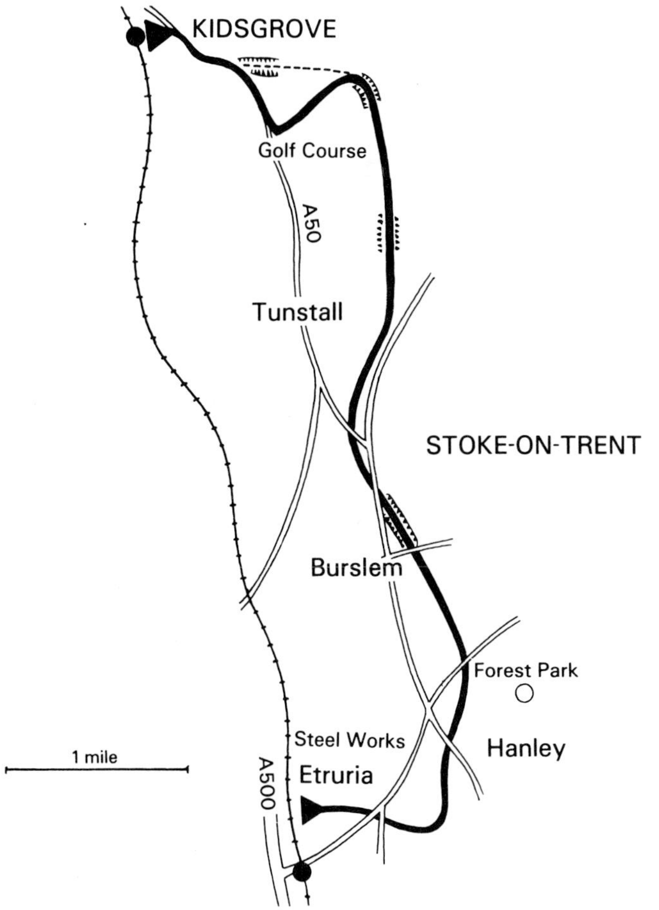

KIDSGROVE

Golf Course

A50

Tunstall

STOKE-ON-TRENT

Burslem

Forest Park

1 mile

Steel Works

A500

Etruria

Hanley

This was, in fact, the old Potteries Loop Line which, as its name suggests, was a loop off the London to Manchester main line. It left the latter in the north at Kidsgrove to take in the Potteries towns before rejoining the main line at Etruria. It was part of the North Staffordshire Railway. 'The Knotty', a line which inspired the sort of local affection that could only be matched by the fierce loyalties of the Great Western enthusiasts. But, while the adherents of the Brunel line regarded their railway as quite simply the best, the 'Knotty' travellers enjoyed theirs for its quirkiness. It was also not a line much addicted to violent change or innovation.

That great chronicler of the Five Towns, Arnold Bennett, wrote a story in which a man returned to the Potteries Loop after an absence of twenty-three years and was delighted to find the timetable unchanged. As Bennett wrote, 'We return Radicals to Parliament but we are proud of a railway which for fine old English conservatism brooks no rival.'

The whole loop has not, in fact, been reclaimed, but it is a good idea to try to walk the whole or as much as possible of its 7 miles as you can manage, though you may meet the obstacles which I encountered. The simplest way to achieve this seems to be to get the train from Etruria to Kidsgrove and then walk back, thereby completing the circle. The train journey lasts only ten minutes, but it is a fascinating little trip. It heads out past the once mighty but now dead Shelton steelworks and stops once at the charming little Jacobean-style station of Middleport and then crosses the startling orange-coloured waters of the Trent and Mersey Canal at Kidsgrove itself. The colour is not, as it appears, pollution from a nearby tomato soup factory but ochre from the Harecastle tunnel through which the canal has just passed. A short walk from the station, across the main A50 road brings the loop line into view. In engineering terms, it is an impressive beginning, a deep cutting partly lined with stone walling. In other ways, even its best friends could not call it immensely attractive, for the line is littered with rusting beer cans, broken bottles, and yellowing newspapers that flutter among the scrub of the cutting floor. Things begin to improve as you move away from the town, and I was beginning to feel slightly happier about the walk when it came to an abrupt end, the way ahead barred by a barbed wire entanglement that would have halted a Panzer division. There was no alternative but to admit defeat and contemplate, not for the first time, the problems that can arise when you choose to follow your own devices. I walked up the main road, keeping an eye on the busy movement of earth-shifting vehicles whose land-reclamation activities had blocked my way. Then at the edge of the city limit, I turned off the road and crossed the golf course to join the cutting that provides an unusual hazard for those whose aim off the tee is inclined to be wayward.

The landscape is surprisingly open with wide views – to the mock ruins on the hill top of Mow Cop to the north and to the tall towers of Stoke to the south. Nearer at hand, is a lumpy landscape of humps and hollows, a man-made landscape for the humps are colliery spoil and the water-filled hollows mining flashes. Land reclamation has made what was black and grimy into green country, but nothing can quite disguise the artificial nature of the scene. The area is known as Goldenhill, which must have been something of a joke, but neighbouring Pittshill at least sounds nearer the mark. It is not by any means an unpleasing area, though the spoil heaps are a popular spot with would-be trials motorcyclists, which means that it is not especially peaceful. But, at Pittshill, it starts to become very pleasant indeed, for this is the start of the fully reclaimed Potteries Greenway. The council have tried, much as their colleagues in North London have tried, to create a country park in an urban setting – and very well they have succeeded too.

Opposite The occupants of these terraced houses in Tunstall were probably not too sad when the 'Knotty' trains stopped running past their back yards. But how attractive these old terraces now look in comparison with the blocks of flats that have replaced so many of them.

The silhouettes that spell out much of the history of Stoke on Trent: on the left, the elegant curves of a pottery bottle kiln; on the right the bulbous chimneys of a foundry.

There has been a lot of planting, but not with the 'municipal park' varieties of exotic species in ordered flower beds, but with the indigenous plants. Dog roses, for example, bloom round many of the bridges as they do on many rural lines where humans have not interfered at all. And they have not tried to pretend that this is really just a country lane – the railway memories have been kept alive through railway relics. At one point a pair of locomotive driving wheels are mounted on a plinth, while the old station yard at Tunstall is graced by a signal, and an engine's smoke box produces a bizarre effect for, seen from a distance, one almost believes that the age of steam has returned to the 'Knotty'.

The railway emphasizes the special nature of Stoke, for it is very clearly a line linking separate communities – Bennett's Five Towns, though there are in fact six of them. It also displays the essential character of the place, running as it does between factories and Victorian terraces. There are still pot works in plenty along the way, though mostly fairly modern buildings. The old terraces are particularly striking. When I first began exploring this region more than a decade ago, it seemed that the old was vanishing at a tremendous rate, and the distant prospect of tower blocks shows what took its place. It is now generally recognized that this was a pretty disastrous policy, not just for Stoke but for many of our old towns – and seeing the well-restored and well-cared-for terraces, you can see why it was a mistake. Conduct a poll today on which people would prefer to live in – terrace or tower – and I would place a good-sized wager on the outcome.

Demolition and rebuilding have had their effect on the line, which tends to disappear at main road crossings, to re-emerge on the other side of the road, but it is never a difficult route to follow. As you go through Burslem, you see something of the old heart of the Potteries, for the unmistakable and elegant shapes of bottle kilns appear above the roof tops. While looking at one of these, which had alongside it the equally distinctive shape of a foundry roof, I was joined by a local out on the Greenway walking his dog. We began to chat about the old line and the industrial region it once served. It is very easy to romanticize old railways and go into raptures about the sinuous curves of bottle kilns, but it is as well to be reminded of the other side of the story. The pot banks, the foundries, and the railway combined to make Stoke a black, grimy place to live. When the ovens were fired, dense smoke covered the town and filled the streets. But if no-one wants those days back, equally, no-one wants them entirely forgotten. The railway, the few preserved kilns – both are eloquent reminders of the old and prosperous days of the region.

The preserved part of the loop ends at Leek New Road and, for the rest of the way, much has been blocked and filled in, though a short section does still lead into Central Forest Park. By a little diligent detective work, it is possible to follow the route back to Etruria, catching regular sightings of the derelict line. It seems fitting in any case to end at Etruria, the site of the first modern potworks in Stoke. It was here beside the Trent and Mersey Canal that Josiah Wedgwood built his works. All that remains is the tiny, circular domed building and, higher up the hill, Etruria Hall, Wedgwood's own house. Stoke has certainly changed in recent years and a walk down the loop shows that change in full measure. It is not perhaps to everyone's taste, though I loved it. But for those who want to escape the urban industrial world the next line should prove very much to their liking.

The Potteries Greenway is notable for the way in which pieces of locomotives dot the route. Here, a locomotive drive wheel seems to have acquired all the qualities of the best modern sculpture.

WADEBRIDGE TO PADSTOW

Route   Wadebridge to Padstow, 5½ miles
Map   OS 200
Access   Wadebridge town centre
             Padstow Station car park
Leaflet Cornwall County Council

Opposite The peaceful waters of the Camel estuary and a distant view of Bodmin Moor beneath threatening clouds. Once the great Atlantic Coast Express thundered along beside the water's edge.

Think of trains to Cornwall and you probably think of the Great Western Railway – well, think again, for this represents the furthest fling of the London and South Western Railway. The distance posts that still dot the line do not inform you how far you are from Paddington but tell you instead of the miles back to Waterloo. The L.S.W.R. never had the romantic image of their arch-rivals the G.W.R. – no charismatic genius to match Brunel, no dramatic crossing of the Tamar, nor, in later years did they have such a brilliant public relations operation, but they were not negligible opponents. They matched the Cornish Riviera Express with the Atlantic Coast Express, headed in its heyday by a mighty Battle of Britain or West Country class locomotive. But, when the Southern Railway became merely the Southern Region, the North Cornish line began to lose ground to its old competitor. Finally, what had become known as the 'withered arm' of the Southern was amputated. The battle for supremacy in Cornwall was ended, and the roar of rival expresses was stilled. Little of those times remains on the line from Wadebridge to Padstow. Its character is not that of battle but of peace and the gentle beauty of a Cornish estuary.

At the Wadebridge end, the walk starts in Eddystone Road, off the A39 and close to the handsome bridge that gives the town its name. The first feeling on setting out is one of slight disappointment. On one side is the estuary of salt flats and mud, gulls and

waders, but the foreground is filled with an unhappy jumble of light industry, the way is tarmacked and leads away to the distant prospect of a construction site. That the plant, on closer inspection, appears to be a new sewage works does little to brighten the picture. Then you pass through a gate, the paved surface gives way to a rough track and Wadebridge is finally abandoned. On that first section it had seemed that the railway engineers had faced few problems, simply laying their tracks on the flat land beside the river – with a slight embankment as protection against floods. But now a hill drops down in a steep slope to the water's edge and the engineers had to blast their way through. Some might find that the cuttings that punctuate this route distract from the pleasure of the walk by literally cutting off the view of the estuary. I cannot agree: on the contrary, they seem to enhance it. The estuary may disappear, but a new world takes its place, a narrow ravine where layers of slate poke through the grass and the abundant wild flowers. Then, when you emerge at the other end, there is the estuary again, but seen fresh and in a new perspective. The world of the cutting and the world of the estuary are total contrasts, not simply because one is enclosed and the other open. The cutting has the brilliance of its flowers and the cosy chatter of land birds – chaffinches are very noticeable among the shrubs and bushes. One of the cuttings seems likely, in early summer, to enjoy a very lively existence, for a small water-filled gully down the side throngs with tadpoles. The estuary offers the distant prospects. Looking back towards the land, you can see the hard outlines of Rough Tor and Brown Willie that crown Bodmin Moor. Out across the water, the raucous gulls wheal above a patiently fishing heron.

The approach to Padstow was blocked by a hill, through which the engineers sliced their way in a deep cutting.

Small boats lie at their moorings in the still waters of Padstow harbour.

Tregunna boasts the one overbridge on the route, built of local stone with a brick-lined arch: but railway reminders are plentiful. The distance posts turn up to check off the mileage back to the station by the Thames; each change of gradient is duly marked and there are the remains of line huts, reduced now to sky-fingering chimneys and rubble. Cornwall may now be thought of principally as a holiday area but, along the way, are reminders not just of the railway past but also of the industrial past. Beyond Tregunna is an extensive area of slate quarrying. The Camel and Penquean quarries appear now as milky lakes surrounded by hills of fragmented slate and the ruins of buildings – but, in their working days, these quarries extended 360 feet (110 metres) below the surface. Slate mining and quarrying may never have held the central place in the local economy held by copper and tin mining, but they were of great importance – and, some miles away at Delabole, the quarry can boast of the largest man-made hole in Britain.

The route bends round, following the line of the river and crosses Oldtown Cove on a high embankment, where a tall bridge allows the water its access to the sea. Across the estuary, small boats speckle the water beneath the high sand dunes of Rock – a favourite place for children who roll down the dunes and play on a beach that shelves very gently into the sea. Beyond that can be seen the distant, tall cliffs of Pentire Point and the Atlantic Ocean. Back on the walk, the track curves again towards the wide inlet of Little Petherick Creek, crossed by a girder bridge – really quite a grand and impressive feature. Beyond that another hill blocks the path, topped by the obelisk of the Jubilee Monument. The railway goes into the deepest of its cuttings to emerge at a stutter of dull bungalows that mark the arrival of Padstow.

Overleaf Padstow at low tide. The line crosses Little Petherick Creek on the girder bridge and then swings round to head towards the town. This photograph was, in fact, taken from the old line itself.

The sad remains of Padstow Station, still suffering indignities at the hands of the demolition workers. Where once the trains steamed in with loads of bucket-and-spade-toting passengers, 'Buses Only' is now the rule.

The end of the walk has a touch of sadness. I arrived to find a demolition gang hacking away at the old station, outside of which – ultimate indignity – was a sign that read 'Buses Only'. Buses Only! where once the mighty steam engine ruled. There is a memory of former glories in the Metropole Hotel which still looks down on the station where its patrons once disembarked with their holiday luggage. And, thank heavens, Padstow itself has not yet lost its old character. In spite of its popularity as a resort, with the inevitable accompaniment of souvenir shops, it remains a working town and a working port. Harbour and fishing boats provide the touch of reality that prevents it from becoming just another twee little picturesque little seaside town. Perhaps all ports look at their best when approached from the sea but, for landlubbers, there can be no better introduction to Padstow than via the old railway from Wadebridge. It might also serve to whet the appetite for a longer and rather more demanding railway walk.

SCARBOROUGH TO WHITBY

Route   Burniston to High Hawsker, 13 miles
Maps   OS 94, 101
Access Burniston via path beside the The Jolly Sailors
            Cloughton Station
            Ravenscar
            Robin Hood's Bay car park
            High Hawsker, by caravan park
Cycling

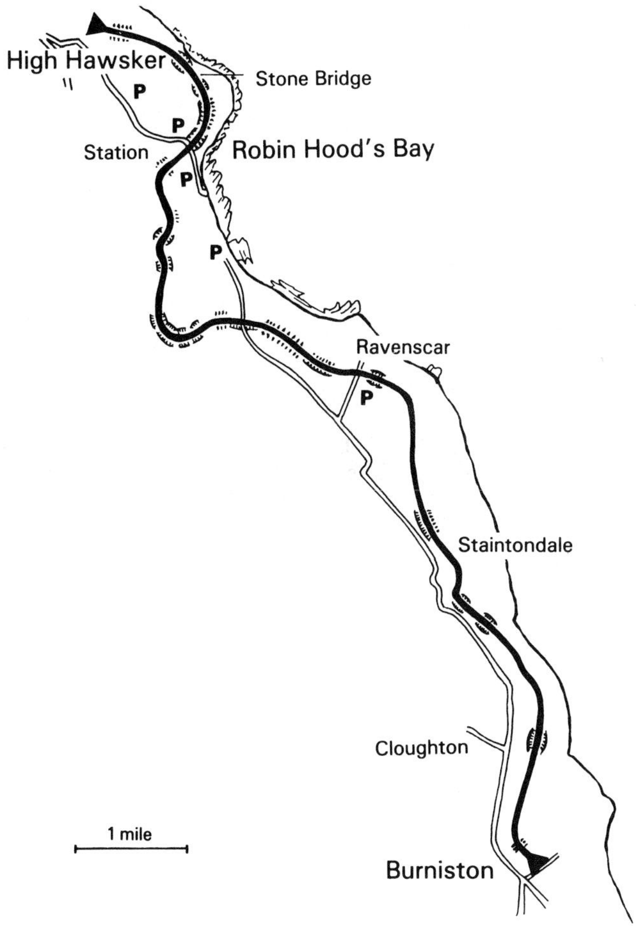

High Hawsker

Stone Bridge

P

P

Station

P

Robin Hood's Bay

P

Ravenscar

P

Staintondale

Cloughton

1 mile

Burniston

This was part of the North Eastern Railway complex, the first of
the many amalgamations of the railway age. The company was
formed out of a group of lines centred around York and around
the person of the railway king, George Hudson. That gentleman,
not noted for scrupulous honesty in his business dealing, was to
spend many of his latter years in lengthy legal wrangles with the
N.E.R., but the empire he founded prospered greatly. Attention

may have been centred on the main line routes, such as those to Scotland and the busy port of Hull but, in happier days, the Scarborough to Whitby line had its full share of the general glory. The concept of the seaside holiday largely owed its existence to the coming of the railways, when new lines linked the populous area of Yorkshire to the coast. The York to Scarborough line was one of the originals in the N.E.R. grouping and, once its success was assured, then it seemed no more than sensible to extend the route northwards to Whitby taking in such picturesque little villages as Robin Hood's Bay. And, if you add to these attractions an excellent source of goods traffic in the alum mines and quarries at Ravenscar, then you have the makings of a highly successful line. And so it proved – until the quarries closed and the motor car and the bus came to replace the train as the favoured means of transport. Walking the line, however, one cannot help mourning what has been lost. Jumping in the car and dashing away can never produce that same sense of mounting excitement that you used to feel as you made your way to the station and waited for the sight of a distant plume of smoke and heard the shrill of the whistle. Then, as you travelled the line, the sea appeared and disappeared along the way, spotted through a gap in the cliffs, removed from view as you plunged into a cutting, tantalizingly close but not yet quite within reach. Something of the old sensations I had enjoyed as a child when I first came to Whitby returned again now.

Although the line ran from Scarborough to Whitby, the walk does not cover the entire route, for the Whitby end has been closed off at the massive viaduct across the Esk, so that the 'official' walk ends short at High Hawsker. The Scarborough end is not especially enticing as it passes through the suburbs, so the recommended route at this end begins at Burniston. One is still left not only with a long walk but with one which encompasses all the best of the very considerable scenic attractions of the area. The two ends are joined by a somewhat irregular bus service which meanders through every hamlet in the region, some delightful scenery and some appetising glimpses of the way one would soon be walking. The bus will drop you off on the edge of High Hawsker and a short stroll past the caravan park – soon, happily, to be lost from view – brings you to the line surfaced in loose ash, which has a certain amount of give underfoot and makes for comfortable if dusty walking. Just a few hundred metres away is the Cleveland Way, offering a cliff-top view for those anxious to make the most of the coastal scenery, but the railway route has its own appeal. A seaside route it may be, but the sea is a regular visitor rather than a constant companion and, to compensate for that, there is some superb moorland scenery and some interesting railway features. The true enthusiast can, of course, always walk down the one and return by the other, scorning the luxury of a bus ride.

The route certainly offers much more than just a trip by the seaside. At once you become aware that this is a very northern landscape with fields divided by straggles of stone walls lolloping across the hills or down the steep slopes that fall away towards the cliffs. The same rugged stonework can be seen on the railway in

Opposite The view from the line at Ravenscar. This lovely stretch of the Yorkshire coast now seems an idyllic spot for holidaymakers, but once the nearby alum mines made this a busy industrial area.

The view across one of the small bridges over a cutting on the Scarborough-Whitby line shows the broad, sweeping curve of Robin Hood's Bay.

culverts and bridges so that there is no feeling that the line is an intrusion into the landscape. It quite definitely belongs. Yet, although there is a sense of belonging, one soon becomes aware that in another sense the line is indeed an intrusion, a level path in an uneven countryside. High embankments cross the deep clefts gouged by the streams hurrying to the sea, while narrow cuttings probe through the rocky hills. The cuts act as drains for the moorland and the stone glistens with water forming a natural habitat for a whole range of rock plants.

The line sweeps out in a wide curve towards Robin Hood's Bay providing, in theory, splendid coastal views, though, if you are unlucky with the weather, the whole east coast may be wrapped in fog and the dreary repetition of a fog horn will be a constant accompaniment to the walk. Down below, the rock shelves, that fold one over the other and stagger down to the sea, are then glimpsed only occasionally in the white foam at the sea's edge. The sea itself appears as a distant, gunmetal sheen. Such conditions are not unusual on this coast. Local cynics will tell you that there are only two forms of weather here. If you escape the fog, you are hit by gales which even affect the landlubbers on the railway where it approaches close to the sea, and it is here at Robin Hood's Bay that it comes as close as anywhere. The resort has become very popular in recent years, its steep streets tumbling down towards the water providing just that picturesque touch that assures it a place on every coach tour for miles around. In season, it is crammed with people, but the railroad misses all that and then itself goes temporarily missing. It has first been domesticated, turned into back gardens – and how very close it must once have been to those houses – and then it has become a car park. Fortunately, it is still easy to follow even though the original

The old station at Cloughton, now a private house. Geese, not steam locomotives, now hiss beside the platform.

bridges have been demolished in road improvement designed for yet more coaches, carrying the trade the railways lost.

The line now runs south through Fylingthorpe – not a bad place to pause for refreshment – and begins a series of convulsive twists to carry itself through the hilly ground up ahead. The railway has turned away from the sea but, for those with a taste for moorland and hill, this is as fine a stretch as any on the entire walk. Cuttings and embankments, steep gradients and sharp curves are all used to force the line through this unpromising country, unpromising that is to the railway engineer. No-one has ever found this an easy landscape, though the farmers who have come here to raise sheep and cattle have made a good job of it. The farms, solid stone, nestle up against the hillside for comfort. The railway cuttings squeeze between the hill farms and snake below the craggy hillside, then, as Ravenscar is approached, the view opens out even wider. The sea appears below while above the hillside is scarred by the old alum quarries.

At Ravenscar itself there is another temporary disappearing act, but the line is soon picked up again where the minor road that runs east from the hotel turns sharply inland. Now the whole character of the route changes again. The moorland now behind him, the railway engineer could relax and take a more straightforward line across level country. It is quiet, tree shaded – and could almost seem tame after the drama of the cliffs. It proves, however, to be no more than an interlude, a pause before the next spectacular. The main feature which gives the line its character is its stance between hills and sea. The streams that drain the upland have carved deep gulleys which, on this section, are all thickly wooded. The line crosses these on high banks so that the walker peers down over the tree tops. It is, or seems to be, a very empty land as far as human activity is concerned, but the wildlife more than compensates. The cries of woodland birds mix with the harsher squawking of the gulls: the sea may be out of sight but it is clearly not far away.

Staintondale boasts one of the two stations surviving along the line, now converted to an attractive private house. It forms a brief interruption to the solitude and peace of the walk which continues now through farm land separated from the sea by a wooded valley in which a busy stream provides a watery accompaniment to the bird song rising from the trees. Then, habitation apears again at the very attractive Hayburn Wyke Hotel. There was a passenger halt here once: you could have gone straight from the train, pausing perhaps for a moment at the hotel, then on down to the bay beyond the woods.

At the wood's end the view opens out again across the fields to the village of Cloughton. Again, the station has become a home, and the line is now occupied by geese and goats. Cloughton is soon followed by Burniston and the end of the line. The route crosses a lane on a bridge at which steps lead down to the land which ends conveniently at the main road and the local pub. That provides just the right finishing touch for a splendid day out. You might feel that the scenery on this line could scarcely be matched anywhere on the railway system, but even this line cannot match our last route for sheer grandeur.

CALLANDER AND GLEN OGLE TRAILS

Route   Callander to Pass of Leny circular walk, 5 miles
            Lochearnhead, Glen Ogle circular walk, 5½ miles
Maps   OS 51, 57
Access   Callander car park
            Lochearnhead
Leaflet Stirling District Council

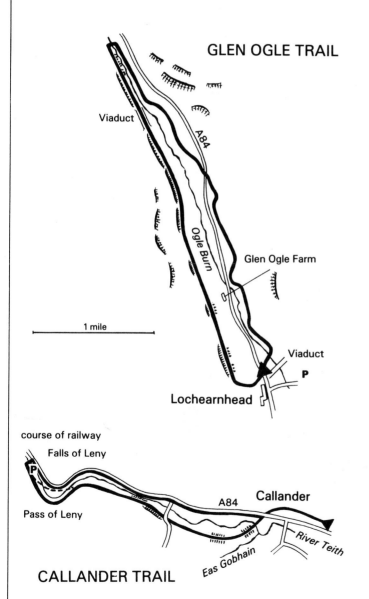

GLEN OGLE TRAIL

Viaduct

A84

Ogle Burn

Glen Ogle Farm

1 mile

Viaduct

P

Lochearnhead

course of railway

Falls of Leny

P

Pass of Leny

A84   Callander

River Teith

Eas Gobhain

CALLANDER TRAIL

This trip has been saved for the last, both because it incorporates what was, in its time, thought of as an important part of one of the major networks, but also because it provides a magnificent route through the heart of the Highlands. One of those reasons would have been sufficient to ensure a place in the book: taken together, the two ensure a place of honour. The line, which was to become an important link in the Caledonian Railway network, joined Stirling to Oban and proved both difficult to build and difficult to keep open once completed: Glen Ogle became known as the Khyber Pass of Scottish railways. Only a few sections have been opened up to walkers, but the two parts described here have quite different characters yet are close enough together for anyone with the necessary transport to walk one in the morning and the other in the afternoon – which is precisely what I did on a memorable day in the Scottish hills.

You can begin your first railway walk at Callander in the unlikely setting of a municipal park of polite hedges and manicured lawns, where only a long lump in the grass gives any hint that trains ever passed this way. Things soon look more promising, however, with the girder bridge over the River Teith, on the far side of which the track is revealed on a low embankment over the river meadows. Nothing very dramatic here, but the route appears to be heading straight for the 2900-foot (882-metre) high peak of Ben Ledi, not one would have thought the ideal direction for a railway to take.

Looking down the Pass of Leny towards Callander. The railway walk beside the river is only just visible as a narrow path through the dense vegetation.

Large rocks sit ominously in the centre of the old trackbed on the Glen Ogle Trail. It was rockfalls as much as anything which caused the closure of this line.

Then one gets closer to the hills and the viewpoint changes; it becomes apparent that there is a gap, albeit a narrow one, between the hills: the Pass of Leny. The engineers would have wasted little time worrying about where to set their line, for the geography of the region dictated the answer. The pass was the only way ahead.

The line here has been very efficiently colonized by birch and sycamore saplings – leaving only the narrowest of gaps for the walker, and the other traffic of the line. When I came along, there was a continuous goods movement in progress, as trains of literally thousands of ants chuntered along loaded with leaves and twigs. The river is glimpsed occasionally through the trees but is never out of earshot, gurgling and splashing down the rocky valley. Route end arrives at the Falls of Leny where only the brick abutments survive to show that this is where the railway crossed the river. The path continues, however, to a footbridge across the river, so that you can, if you wish, cross over and return to Callander on the opposite bank. It makes for a pleasant morning stroll, with a tantalizing first taste of Highland scenery. It is an appropriate prelude to the grander theme which is to follow.

The next stage of the journey is through Glen Ogle and begins at Lochearnhead. A waymarked route leads away from the western side of the A84 to join the line cut into the flank of the 2162-foot (657-metre) hill, Sgarrach Nuadh. The route follows the contour of the hill at approximately the 1000-foot (300-metre) level so that, throughout its length, it stands high above the valley floor and offers quite splendid views of the Highlands – and you do not have

Overleaf In any other setting the viaduct in Glen Ogle would be a dominant feature in the landscape, but here it is almost over- whelmed by the magnifi- cence of the Highland scenery.

to be a patriotic Scot to believe that this is scenery as splendid as you will find anywhere in the world. Even before you start climbing up the track, you have no difficulty in picking out the line of the railway. It appears as a strip of trees, running the length of the glen. Seeds drifting into the glen have very little chance of settling on the steep slopes and, even when they do, have even less chance of evading the ever-chomping jaws of the hill sheep. But the fenced-off, level ground of the railway is a very different matter and so the railway is seen as an elongated wood above the valley floor.

Once on the line, attention is divided – agreeably divided it must be said – between the fascination of the line itself and the majesty of the surrounding scenery. Look down across the glassy waters of Loch Earn and, even in early May, the distant hills are still patched with snow. The glen itself runs northward, a narrow pass between high hills leading to still higher hills in the distance. It is a place to pause and simply look, taking in the rich colours, the golden brown of bracken in the sun, the dark green of turf, the more ominous shades of the harsh rock edges that form the skyline. The rail enthusiast's eye will also be caught by the distant sighting of the viaduct that leads a branch line along the northern shore of Loch Earn, an encouragement to turn to matters closer at hand. It is immediately apparent that the building of the Glen Ogle line was an immense undertaking, every fraction of the way having to be blasted out of the hillside. Here it was not just a question of completing the line and then sitting back with a feeling of self-satisfaction, for building the line proved only to be the first of the difficulties. The real problems came with trying to keep it open. Not surprisingly, the weather brought many hazards, as winds funnelled up the pass and piled snow into deep drifts. On a memorable Friday in March 1881, the night mail set out up the glen, heading for Oban. It reached its destination the following Tuesday, after the passengers had spent three miserable, shivering nights stuck in the freezing coaches. Summer, too, could bring its problems, for the mountain showed a disturbing tendency to slip in wet weather – and the walker soon finds evidence of this activity in quite massive boulders that have lodged in the middle of the track. Falling rocks were dramatic, but rare, events on the line – but landslips were all too common. Every effort was made to stabilize the land beside the line and, at many places, you can see the strongly buttressed walls set against the hillside. Safety was a constant preoccupation, and trip wires were installed which triggered off the signal system to close the section when a fall occurred. It was one such major fall that finally brought the working life of the line to an end.

There is no need to contemplate the worries of railway engineers when walking the line, though there is no escaping the evidence of the railway past, for the rough ballast makes itself felt through even the stoutest boots. It seems a small price to pay for such a truly delightful walk. The eye is constantly beguiled by sights both near and far: by the glimpse of a tall peak between the rounded hills, or the broken rock left as a miniature peak where the engineers have blasted a way through for the railway. There is one spot where the engineering dominates all, the one big viaduct that strides across the hillside cleft, demanding attention. Here, too, the customary screen of trees is broken, offering the widest views found on the whole route. It is a wonderful conjunction of engineering marvel and perfect viewpoint, and one can well understand why excursion trains along this route were always popular.

Half a mile further on, the line disappears into a deep rock cutting which is now more like a river than a railway, for all the water from the hills seems to have collected here. This is, inevitably, the end of the railway part of the walk, but not the end of the trail itself. That turns back to Lochearnhead via Major Cauldfield's military road, part of the network of roads begun by General Wade, after the uprising of 1745. It then continues on a

Seen close to, the massive nature of the Glen Ogle viaduct becomes clear. It is clear, too, why the men who had to build the line christened this glen 'The Khyber Pass of Scottish Railways'.

Looking down on Loch Earn from the Glen Ogle Trail. The viaduct down by the loch carried the old Caledonian Railway line to Crieff. It closed in 1951. Here, perhaps, is a candidate for another railway walk.

far older route, the drove road which was first used six centuries ago by farmers from the hills bringing their sheep and cattle to the markets in the south. Here, below the railway, generations of road makers have made their ways through the glen: the cattle picking their route, little concerned about gradients and surfaces; the military, with quite different requirements, needing to be certain of getting horses and wheeled vehicles through the pass, and following a convoluted route on the valley floor, and finally the modern road engineers, prepared to take a direct route through the glen. Each generation has had its own problems, and found its own solutions and, from the military road and the drove road, you can look across to the work of the railway engineers, who faced the most difficult problems of all. The viaduct stands as a fitting memorial to their triumph. There is perhaps a touch of sadness in the thought of so much effort, so much endeavour now apparently wasted. No steam whistle now echoes round the glen, no puffing, panting locomotive toils up the gradients. Yet the line remains, as so many old lines remain, for us to enjoy. Each year more and more routes are being adopted for use by walkers and cyclists; each year more and more people are coming to appreciate their special appeal. If you can no longer stop at the end of the glen and buy a four-and-sixpenny ticket to Glasgow, you can travel the line with no expense other than that of a little muscle power. The delights of the glen and the majesty of the railway are still there to be enjoyed, just as so many other old tracks remain for future generations who will come to walk the line.

GAZETTEER

The following walks have all been designated as walkways by local authorities.
Maps: the numbers given refer to the 1:50 000 Ordnance Survey maps.
C indicates that cycling is possible on the route.
L a leaflet is available describing the route. These leaflets are supplied by the county council unless otherwise stated.
Numbers in *italics* refer to the map on page 52.

ENGLAND

AVON

Bath to Bristol (10 miles)
Map 172   C
(*see* page 119)
1 **Cheddar Valley Railway Walk: Cheddar to Yatton** (10 miles)
Maps 172, 182   C   L (Woodspring District Council)
2 **Radstock to Midsomer Norton** (2 miles)
Footpath runs from map reference ST 688549 to ST 658529
Map 183

BEDFORDSHIRE

3 **Stevington Country Walk: Stevington to Bromham** (2 miles)
Map 153   L

BUCKINGHAMSHIRE

Newport Pagnell Branch: Newport Pagnell to Wolverton
(4 miles)
Map 152
(*see* page 143)

CHESHIRE

4 **Mow Cop Trail: Rushton to Mow Cop** (9 miles)
Part of trail only on railway. *See also* STAFFORDSHIRE
Map 118   L
5 **The Middlewood Way: Middlewood to Bollington** (8 miles)
Map 118   L
6 **The Whitegate Way: Catsclough to Cuddington** (6 miles)
Maps 117, 118   L
Wirral Way, West Kirby to Hooton (12 miles)
Maps 108, 117   L
(*see* page 130)

CLEVELAND

7 **Guisborough Branch Walkway: Morton Grange Farm to Bousdale Woods** (3 miles)
Map 93   L
8 **Castle Eden Walkway: Thorpe Thewles to Wynyard** (3½ miles)
Map 93   L

9 **Eston/Normanby Branch Footpaths: South Bank to Parkway A174** (2 miles)
Map 93

CORNWALL
Wadebridge to Padstow (5½ miles)
Map 200   L
(*see* page 158)

CUMBRIA
10 **Alston to County Boundary** (1½ miles)
Map 86
11 **Brampton to Brampton Junction** (1½ miles)
Map 86
12 **Coniston to Torver** (3 miles)
Map 97

DERBYSHIRE
High Peak Trail: Cromford to Hurdlow (17½ miles)
Map 119   L (Peak National Park and Derbyshire CC)   C
(*see* page 62)
Manifold Track (*see* STAFFORDSHIRE)
13 **Monsal Trail: Bakewell to Blackwell** (8 miles)
Map 119   L (Peak National Park)
14 **Sett Valley Trail: New Mills to Hayfield** (2½ miles)
Map 110   L   C
15 **Tibshelf to Holmewood Trail** (4 miles)
Map 120
Tissington Trail, Ashbourne to Parsley Hay (13 miles)
Map 119   L (Peak National Park)   C
(*see* page 70)

DEVON
16 **Braunton to Barnstaple** (6½ miles)
Map 180   C
17 **Bovey Tracey to Wooleigh** (1½ miles)
Map 191   C
18 **Ilfracombe to Bickerbridge** B3231 (3½ miles)
Map 180   C
19 **Tiverton to Great Western Canal** (2½ miles)
Map 181

DURHAM
20 **Brandon to Bishop Auckland** (9½ miles)
Map 93   L   C
21 **Deerness Valley Walk: Broompark to Crook** (7 miles)
Maps 88, 92   L   C
Derwent Walk: Shotley Bridge to Swalwell (10½ miles)
Map 88   L   C
(*see* page 86)
22 **Lanchester Valley Walk: Broompark to Bearpark** (12 miles)
Map 88   L   C
Waskerley Way: Meeting Slacks to Consett (7 miles)
Maps 87, 88   L   C
(*see* page 86)

ESSEX
23   **Braintree to Dunmow** (7 miles)
     Map 167

GLOUCESTERSHIRE
     Stroud Valleys Trail: Stonehouse to Nailsworth (6 miles)
     Map 162   L   C
     (*see* page 124)
24   **Cotswold Water Park: Cricklade to South Cerney** (3 miles)
     Map 163   L

GREATER MANCHESTER
25   **Red Rock Railway: Standish to Adlington** (2 miles)
     Map 108   C
26   **Whelley Loop: Standish to Wigan** (3 miles)
     Map 108   C

HAMPSHIRE
27   **Gosport to Fareham Line: Bridgemary to Alverstoke** (3½ miles)
     Map 196   C
28   **Hayling Railway Track: Langstone to South Hayling** (3 miles)
     Map 197
29   **Meon Valley Line: Wickham to West Meon** (9 miles)
     Maps 185, 196   C
30   **Test Valley Line: Fullerton to Mottisfont** (7 miles)
     Map 185   C

HERTFORDSHIRE
31   **Ayot Greenway: Ayot Green to Blackbridge** (2½ miles)
     Map 166   L
32   **Cole Green Way: Cole Green to Hertford Viaduct** (2 miles)
     Map 166   L   C

HUMBERSIDE
33   **Hudson Way: Beverley to Market Weighton** (10 miles)
     Maps 106, 107
34   **Hull to Hornsea** (10 miles)
     Map 107
35   **Selby-Driffield Line: Market Weighton to Bubwith** (8½ miles)
     Map 106

ISLE OF WIGHT
36   **Freshwater to Yarmouth** (2 miles)
     Map 196
37   **Newport to Cowes** (3½ miles)
     Map 196
38   **Newport to Wootton** (2 miles
     Map 196
39   **Shanklin to Wroxhall** (2 miles)
     Map 196   C

LANCASHIRE
40   **Lune Walk: Glasson to Bull Beck** (12 miles)
     Maps 97, 102   L   C
41   **Healey Dell Nature Trail: Rochdale** (3 miles)
     Map 109

LINCOLNSHIRE
42   **Spa Trail: Woodhall Spa to Horncastle** (7 miles)
Map 122   L

LONDON
Parkland Walk: Finsbury Park to Alexandra Palace (4 miles)
Map 176   L
(*see* page 148)

MERSEYSIDE
43   **Rainford Linear Park: St Helens** (2 miles)
Map 108
Wirral Way (*see* CHESHIRE)

NORFOLK
44   **Marriotts Way: Hellesdon to Attlebridge** (7 miles)
Map 133
Weavers' Way: Blickling to Stalham (15 miles)
Map 133   L
(*see* page 94)

NOTTINGHAMSHIRE
45   **Southwell Trail: Farnsfield to Southwell** (4½ miles)
Map 120   L

STAFFORDSHIRE
46   **Biddulph Valley Way: Congleton to Biddulph** (4 miles)
Map 118
47   **Churnet Valley Railway: Leek to County Boundary** (7 miles);
48   **Kingswinford Branch Railway Walk: Wolverhampton to Dudley**
(5½ miles) continues as Valley Park Walk (*see* WEST MIDLANDS)
Map 139   L (South Staffs District Council)
Manifold Track: Waterhouses to Hulme End (8½ miles)
Map 119   L (Peak National Park)   C
(*see* page 100)
Potteries Greenway: Kidsgrove to Hanley (7 miles)
Map 118   C
(*see* page 153)

SUFFOLK
49   **Hadleigh Railway Walk: Hadleigh Old Station to 1 mile north of
Rayburn** (2½ miles)
Map 155   L
50   **Lavenham Walk** (1½ miles)
Map 155   L
51   **Valley Walk: Rodbridge to Sudbury** (2½ miles)
Map 155   L   C

SURREY
52   **Downs Link: St Martha's Hill, Guildford to Steyning** (30 miles)
Maps 186, 187, 198   L   C

SUSSEX, EAST

Forest Way: East Grinstead to Groombridge (9½ miles)
Maps 187, 188   L   C
(*see* page 136)

53   **Hailsham to Hellingly** (2 miles)
Map 199

SUSSEX, WEST

Downs Link (*see* SURREY)
Worth Way: East Grinstead to Three Bridges (6 miles)
Map 187   L   C
(*see* page 136)

TYNE AND WEAR

54   **Wylam and Walbottle Waggonways: Wylam Bridge to Black Callerton** (4½ miles)
Map 88   L   C

WARWICKSHIRE

55   **Weddington Country Walk: Nuneaton to Ashby** (1½ miles)
Map 140   L

WEST MIDLANDS

56   **Berkswell to Kenilworth** (4½ miles)
Maps 139, 140

57   **Harborne Walkway: Harborne to Summerfield Park** (2 miles)
Map 139

58   **Valley Park Walk: Aldersley to Castlecroft** (1½ miles)
Map 139

59   **West Bromwich Parkway: West Bromwich to Wednesbury** (2½ miles)
Map 139   L   C

YORKSHIRE, NORTH

60   **Ingleby Greenhow to Farndale Moor** (6½ miles) (section of Lyke Wake Walk)
Map 94
Scarborough to Whitby (13 miles)
Maps 94, 101   C
(*see* page 165)

YORKSHIRE, WEST

61   **Garforth to Kippax** (2 miles)
Map 105

62   **Newmillerdam to Chevet Lane** (2 miles)
Map 111

SCOTLAND

BORDERS

63   **Galashiels, Torwoodley to Tweedbank** (3½ miles)
Map 73   C

CENTRAL

64   **Denny to Fankerton** (2 miles)
Maps 64, 65   C
The Callander Trail: circular walk via Pass of Leny (5 miles)
Map 57
(*see* page 171)
Glen Ogle Trail: circular route from Lochearnhead (5½ miles)
Map 51   L
(*see* page 171)
65   **Tillicoultry to Dollar** (3 miles)
Map 58

FIFE

66   **Boblingen Way: Glenrothes, Woodside to Leslie** (3½ miles)
Map 59   C

GRAMPIAN

67   **Old Deeside Line Walk: Aberdeen to Peterculter** (7 miles)
Map 38   C
68   **Cambus O'May to Ballater** (4 miles)
Map 37
69   **Speyside Way: Ballindalloch to Craigellachie** (13 miles)
Map 28   L (Moray District Council)   C

LOTHIAN

Pencaitland Walk: West Saltoun to Crossgatehall (6½ miles)
Map 66   L (East Lothian District Council)   C
(*see* page 105)
70   **Water of Leith Walkway: Slateford to Juniper Green** (3 miles)
Map 66   L (Edinburgh District Council)   C

STRATHCLYDE

71   **Irvine to Knockentiber** (4 miles)
Map 70   C
72   **Kilmacolm to Bardrainney** (2½ miles)
Map 63
73   **Kirkintilloch to Millers Neuk** (1½ miles)
Map 64   C

WALES

DYFED

74   **Cynheidre to Cefneithin** (12 miles)
Map 159
75   **Gwendraeth Railway: from B4308 2 miles east of Kidwelly to Drefach** (15½ miles)
Map 159

GLAMORGAN, MID-

76   **Dare Valley Country Park Industrial Trail, Aberdare** (2 miles)
Map 170   L (Park Warden)

Penydarren Tramway: Abercynon to Pont y Gwaith (3 miles)
Maps 170, 171
(*see* page 58)
77   **Pontypridd to Nantgarw** (3½ miles)
Map 171   C

GLAMORGAN, WEST
78   **Abergwynfi to Cymmer** (2½ miles)
Map 170   C
79   **Bryn to Port Talbot** (3½ miles)
Map 170
80   **Durwant to Swansea** (5 miles)
Map 159   C
81   **Glyncorrwg to Afan Argoed Country Park** (6½ miles)
Map 170   C
82   **Pontrhydyfen to Blaengwynfi** (6 miles)
Map 170   C
83   **Port Talbot to Cwmafan** (2 miles)
Map 170   C

GWENT
Wye Valley Walk: Tintern Parva and Whitebrook to Redbrook
(6 miles)
Map 162   L
(*see* page 111)

GWYNEDD
84   **Lake Padarn Walk, Llanberis: circular walk partly on railway**
(5 miles)
Map 115   L
85   **Morfa Mawddach Walk: Morfa Mawddach to Penmaenpool**
(5 miles)
Map 124   L (Snowdonia National Park)
86   **Port Penrhyn to Bethesda** (5 miles)
Map 155   L   (Gwynedd Cycle Routes)   C

USEFUL ADDRESSES

The following organizations are especially concerned with walking
and cycling on old railways:

Branch Line Society
N J Hill
73 Norfolk Park Avenue
Sheffield S2 2RB

Railway Path Project, Cyclebag
35 King Street
Bristol BS1 4DZ

The Railway Ramblers
6 Cherville Court
Mill Lane
Romsey
Hants SO5 8EX

**Scottish Railway Path and Cycle
Route Project**
180 High Street
Edinburgh EH1 1QS

**'Spokes'
The Lothian Cycle Campaign**
53 George IV Bridge
Edinburgh   EH1 1EJ

TRAVEL AND ACCOMMODATION

Information on accommodation and local bus and train services is most easily obtained by contacting tourist information centres. The following is a list of information centres in towns close to the walks listed in this book. A full list of all the centres in Britain with details of the services provided can be found in the *Directory of Tourist Information Centres* published by the English Tourist Board, 4 Grosvenor Gardens, London SW1 0DU (telephone 01 730 3400).

ENGLAND

AVON
Bath, Abbey Churchyard
Bristol, Colston House, Colston Street

BEDFORDSHIRE
Bedford, 10 St Pauls Square

BUCKINGHAMSHIRE
Milton Keynes, Midsummer House, 425–427 Midsummer Boulevard

CHESHIRE
Congleton, Town Hall, High Street
Knutsford, Council Offices, Toft Road
Macclesfield, Town Hall, Market Place

CLEVELAND
Middlesborough, 125 Albert Road

CORNWALL
Bodmin, Shire House, Mount Folly Square

CUMBRIA
Alston, The Railway Station
Brampton, Moot Hall, Market Place

DERBYSHIRE
Alfreton, Alfreton Library, Severn Square
Ashbourne, 13 The Market Place
Bakewell, Old Market Hall
Buxton, The Crescent
Matlock Bath, The Pavilion

DEVON
Barnstaple, 20 Holland Street
Bovey Tracey, Lower Car Park
Ilfracombe, The Promenade
Exeter, Civil Centre, Dix's Field

DURHAM

West Auckland, Old Manor House Hotel, Front Street

ESSEX

Colchester, Town Hall, High Street

GLOUCESTERSHIRE

Cirencester, Corn Hall, Market Place
Stroud, Council Offices, High Street

GREATER MANCHESTER

Bolton, Town Hall
Oldham, Local Studies Library, 84 Union Street

HAMPSHIRE

Gosport, Ferry Gardens
Hayling Island, 32 Seafront
Petersfield, The Library, 27 The Square
Romsey, Bus Station Car Park, Broadwater Road

HERTFORDSHIRE

Hertford, Vale House, 43 Cowbridge

HUMBERSIDE

Beverley, 30 Saturday Market
Hull, Central Library, Albion Street

ISLE OF WIGHT

Cowes, 1 Bath Road
Newport, 21 High Street
Shanklin, 67 High Street
Yarmouth, Quay Road

KENT

Tunbridge Wells, Town Hall

LANCASHIRE

Lancaster, 7 Dalton Square

LINCOLNSHIRE

Woodhall Spa, Jubilee Park, Stixwould Road

LONDON

Harrods, Knightsbridge, SW1
Selfridges, Oxford Street, W1
Victoria, Victoria Station Forecourt, SW1

MERSEYSIDE

Birkenhead, Reference Library, Borough Road
Liverpool, 29 Lime Street

NORFOLK

Norwich, Augustine Steward House, 14 Tombland
Walsingham, Shire Hall Museum, Common Place, Little Walsingham

NOTTINGHAMSHIRE
Newark, The Ossington, Beast Market Hill, Castlegate

SOMERSET
Cheddar, The Library, Union Street
Shepton Mallet, 7 Market Place

STAFFORDSHIRE
Leek, New Stockwell House, Stockwell Street
Stoke on Trent, Central Library, Bethesda Street, Hanley

SUFFOLK
Sudbury, Library, Market Hill

SURREY
Guildford, The Civic Hall, London Road

SUSSEX, EAST
Hailsham, Area Library, Western Road
Hove, Town Hall, Norton Road

SUSSEX, WEST
Arundel, 61 High Street

TYNE AND WEAR
Gateshead, Central Library, Prince Consort Road
Newcastle, Central Library, Princess Square

WARWICKSHIRE
Kenilworth, The Library, 11 Smalley Place
Nuneaton, Nuneaton Library, Church Street

WEST MIDLANDS
Birmingham, 2 City Arcade
Dudley, 39 Churchill Precinct

YORKSHIRE, NORTH
Danby, Danby Lodge National Park Centre
Scarborough, St Nicholas Cliff
Whitby, New Quay Road

YORKSHIRE, WEST
Leeds, Central Library, Calverley Street
Wakefield, Town Hall, Wood Street

SCOTLAND

BORDERS
Galashiels, Bank Street

CENTRAL
Bannockburn
Callander, Leny Road

Killin, Main Street
Tillicoultry, Clock Mill, Upper Mill Street

FIFE

Kirkcaldy, Esplanade

GRAMPIAN

Aberdeen, St Nicholas House, Broad Street
Ballater, Station Square
Dufftown, The Square

LOTHIAN

Edinburgh, Waverley Market
Pencraig, A1 East Linton

STRATHCLYDE

Greenock, Municipal Buildings, 23 Clyde Square
Kilmarnock, Civic Centre
Troon, Municipal Buildings, South Beach

WALES

DYFED

Carmarthen, Lammas Street
Pont Abraham, Service Area, Junction 49, M4

GLAMORGAN, MID-

Merthyr Tydfil, Brecon Mountain Railway, Pont Station

GLAMORGAN, WEST

Aberavon, Council Offices
Neath, Aberdulais Car Park
Swansea, Singleton Street

GWENT

Tintern, Tintern Abbey

GWYNEDD

Dolgellau, The Bridge
Llanberis

FURTHER READING

Further Information on Old Railways

Wignall, C J. 1983. *Complete British Railways Map and Gazetteer from 1830–1981*. Oxford Publishing Company, Poole.

The series, 'Forgotten Railways' (David and Charles) can be recommended.

General Reading on the Physical Appearance of Railways

Binney, Marcus and Pearce, David. 1979. *Railway Architecture*. Orbis, London.
Ransom, P J G. 1981. *The Archaeology of Railways*. World's Work.

Reports on Proposals for Old Lines

Appleton, J H. 1970. *Disused Railways in the Countryside of England and Wales*. HMSO, London.
Grimshaw, John. 1972. *Disused Railway Lines in Scotland*. HMSO, London.
Grimshaw, John, 1982. *Study of Disused Railway Lines in England and Wales*. HMSO, London.

General Guides to British Landscape, Scenery, and Wildlife

Hoskins, W G. 1977. *The Making of the English Landscape* (2nd ed.). Hodder & Stoughton, London.
Muir, Richard. 1981. *Shell Guide to Reading the Landscape*. Michael Joseph, London.

INDEX

Numbers in *italics* refer to illustrations